The Navy That
Crossed Mountains

The Navy That
Crossed Mountains

Martín López was a sixteenth-century carpenter of Spain who joined the Cortés expedition to Mexico. He longed to become an adventurous swordsman, and he did. But it was his carpentry that was one of the greatest factors in the defeat of the Aztecs. Centuries before the word "prefabricated" was coined, López designed a prefabricated navy. He built thirteen ships, disassembled them, and had the parts carried across the tortuous mountain route to the huge lake fronting the capital city of Moctezuma. Reassembled, the little navy was indispensable in the storming of Tenochtitlán.

The Navy That Crossed Mountains

By James Norman

Illustrated by Dirk Gringhuis

G. P. Putnam's Sons   New York

For

Melissa Thompson

Published simultaneously in the Dominion of
Canada by Longmans Canada Limited
Library of Congress Catalog Card Number:
63-15578

MANUFACTURED IN THE UNITED
STATES OF AMERICA

12216

Third Impression

Contents

The Navy That
Crossed Mountains

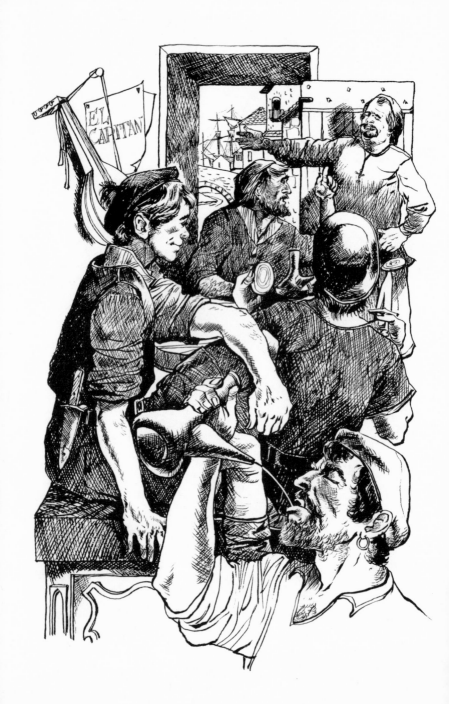

1 : Apprentice Adventurer

He was a wiry, spade-bearded young adventurer, as skilled with the sword as he was with the saw. Partly because of his sword, but mostly because of his proficiency with carpenter's tools, Spain conquered the New World when she did—yet, today, the name of this man who had so much to do with the success of the conquest is hardly known.

The name is Martín López, that of a man who should be credited with some of the most remarkable firsts in the history of high adventure.

Martín López built the first navy on the American continent. He carried his ships over ten-thousand-foot-high mountain passes in order to capture one of the world's largest and richest imperial cities. He commanded his tiny fleet in the most significant naval actions in the history of the Western Hemisphere; naval actions that took place a mile and a half above sea level, almost two hundred miles from the sea, on a lake which today has completely disappeared.

Four hundred years before our own modern naval

engineers thought of prefabricating ships at secure inland points, as they did during World War II, then transporting them overland to a launching port, Martín did just that.

Martín López' story has a beginning that rings a little like that of any young man in any age. He wanted adventure.

He was born in Sevilla, Spain, a city of romance and fanciful architecture left by the Moors who had just been driven from Spain. But Sevilla, during Martín's boyhood, was more than a place of vivid memories of wars against the Saracens. Three years after Martín was born in 1489, Christopher Columbus discovered some far-off islands and Sevilla became the great port from which expedition after expedition sailed to the New World.

It is hard for us, familiar as we are from childhood with most remote places and names on the globe, to picture the feelings of young men who lived in Martín López' time. It was an age of romance and adventure. The oceans were gateways to unknown worlds. Columbus had opened the doors, revealing glimpses of a mysterious and glorious world. The lush tropical lands, the strange people and the perils of exploration excited the imagination of everyone.

As a boy, Martín listened to the tales of chivalry and adventure. He played with other lads along the waterfront of Sevilla which straddled the Guadalquivir River which flowed into the Atlantic. He watched the ships returning from distant seas. He and his friends heard sailors spin tales of fabulous adventures; how they had explored the Bay of Honduras and the tropical shore of Darien. Martín met a sailor who had followed Nuñez de Balboa, climbing across the mighty barrier of the Isthmus of Panama to gaze down upon the Pacific Ocean.

Martín López' dreams were like those of almost every boy and man in Sevilla—dreams of the New World, of romance and riches. Martín believed so firmly he would eventually seek his fortune in the mysterious lands to the west that as a boy he even prepared himself for this.

He learned swordsmanship. He became adept with the crossbow, learning how to string the cords, to adjust the tension nut and to fire accurately. He learned to ride. He did all this secretly and in spare moments. There was a good reason for the secrecy—his father.

Martín's father, Don Xriptóual Díaz López, was one of the few unromantic men in Sevilla. The New World did not appeal to him. He had no intention of letting his sons leave the family business while money was pouring in. Xriptóual was a carpenter and shipwright. For years he had struggled along without great success, but now there was a shipbuilding boom in Sevilla.

He was growing wealthy constructing and outfitting ships for the flourishing trade with the newly settled Caribbean islands. As each of his four sons grew of age, he put them to work shipbuilding. At thirteen Martín was already learning his father's trade.

The work bored young Martín. He had his heart set on distant horizons. Once, at the age of fifteen, he tried to run away. A fleet built by his father and under the command of Alonzo Quintero was about to sail for the Canaries and the Caribbean. Martín hid himself aboard one of the vessels. He was discovered by Quintero, a friend of Don Xriptóual, and was put ashore.

Aboard the same ship was another nineteen-year-old lad with whom Martín would eventually share one of the world's most memorable adventures. The youthful cavalier aboard Quintero's flagship was Hernando Cortés of Medellin—a youngster who had studied briefly at the University of Salamanca because his father had wanted him to become a lawyer. Like Martín, he preferred adventuring in the New World where gold and glory might be won.

When Martín's father learned of his son's misadventure, he administered a severe whipping. That night he lectured all his sons.

"Let the wastrels go to the Indies," he said. "Your place is here beside me. Your fortune is here in shipbuilding. Learn your trade well, my sons, it will carry you farther than the sword."

Although Martín's older brothers shared his romantic dreams, none was as spirited and stubborn as the boy. They remained silent, letting Martín talk.

"My brothers are older," Martín told his father. "They will inherit your business. I want to seek my fortune on Hispanola."

Don Xriptóual flared up, replying, "It is but a false dream. Make your fortune here, Son."

"But Father, I want to see the new lands."

"Son, it requires much money to adventure abroad," said the father. "One must be properly equipped. One must supply one's own food and other needs for a long voyage. You can't set out with nothing. You also need the connections and protection of a patron."

"But we aren't poor."

"No, my son. I'll hear nothing of it now. Learn your trade. When you reach the age of twenty-five we shall discuss your place. Until then, mind your chores."

For ten more years Martín obeyed his father. He labored in the shipyards, learning to trim timbers, to set keels, to fit rudders, and to do the thousand and one details of cabinetwork. However, in his spare moments he practiced swordsmanship. He had become the owner of a fine Toledo steel blade. At night, instead of courting girls as his father and his mother, Doña Estebanya, desired, he frequented the inns where sailors passed their shore leave. He never tired of their lively stories of voyages to the Indies.

By the time Martín was a young man a good deal had been learned about the distant islands and some of the shores of the New World which Spanish explorers still believed to be the Indies. The coast of South America had been skirted as far as the Río de la Plata. The Bahama islands had been explored. The Englishman, Cabot, had sailed from Labrador to Florida. Nevertheless, there were still many gaps.

Although the Carribean islands had been explored and colonies settled on them, and though the beaches of North and South America had been traced, the shores of the great Mexican Gulf, sweeping deeply westward, remained concealed from the eyes of the navigator. It was time, now, for the rich realms of Mexico to be discovered.

At the age of twenty-five, Martín López—obedient all these years—again approached his father concerning his family rights and his desire to leave home. Once more there was a family conference in the Spanish manner, that is, of father, sons and some male relatives. The men gathered in the huge family kitchen. Candles glowed and red wine was served.

Martín was now a handsome, muscular lad. He was

five feet ten in height, had a dark, spade beard, a ready smile and a quick wit. He was a favorite of Don Xriptóual. However, though the father admired his son's persistence, he still refused to give his blessing to any project of adventure. Don Xriptóual had something else in mind.

Martín's father had made some inquiries about the islands. They were becoming settled. Colonists were beginning to farm and mine. Business was being conducted. Grants of land and Indian serfs were being awarded to those who would settle down and work. To receive any of these benefits one had to have certain political connections as well as enough money to get started.

"There are new settlements on the island called Fernandella," said the father. "They offer opportunities. I have written to Pánfilo de Narvaez who is the chief lieutenant of Don Diego Velasquez, the governor of that island. He tells me he will be your patron. You will be awarded land near the port of Trinidad where Don Pánfilo says you can farm and do carpentry. You must take tools. When you go there two of my men, the brothers Pedro and Miguel de Mafla, shall accompany you as servants. Your cousin, Juan Martinez Narices, also wishes to go with you."

Thus, in the year 1516, the young man who was to become Hernando Cortés' key in the conquest of the

Aztec empire sailed for the New World. He went, not as a swashbuckling cavalier as he had hoped, but as an artisan commissioned to set up a branch of his father's carpentry business on a remote island called Fernandella—now known as Cuba.

Martín traveled aboard a Spanish caravel which weathered severe storms and delays in crossing the Atlantic. Following more than three months of hardship the voyagers put in at San Jago on the southeast coast of Cuba. Although it was a small settlement, San Jago was the seat of the island government.

Immediately upon landing, Martín López went to the house of the governor, where he met Don Pánfilo Narvaez and presented his father's sealed letter of introduction.

Narvaez was an arrogant man and he left a bad impression on Martín.

"What do you do?" Narvaez asked coldly.

Martín had already heard in the village that Governor Velasquez was outfitting a fleet to be commanded by Hernandez de Cordova. It was said the fleet would explore the mysterious regions to the west.

"I wish to go on the Cordova expedition," Martín said. "My sword is at the governor's disposal." He rested his hand on the hilt of his Toledo blade which, as yet, had never drawn blood.

Narvaez opened the letter from Sevilla. He frowned

as he read it. "Why didn't you say that your saw, not your sword, is at the governor's disposal?" he said with irony.

"I would prefer going with Cordova."

Narvaez shook his head. "Hernandez de Cordova has all the fighting men he needs," he said. "Trades are needed on the island. Your saw and adze will be more useful. I shall take you to the governor."

"I do not wish to carpenter."

"You have the look of a carpenter, not of a soldier," Narvaez replied contemptuously.

Again, Martín's hand moved toward the hilt of his sword. Then he paused. Although he was fearless, he resisted the urge to draw the weapon. He was level-headed enough to avoid a foolish duel which would help him in no way. Someday the sword which he kept sheathed was to put an end to Narvaez' arrogant career. That engagement would take place in a distant land, atop an Indian temple.

He let himself be led into the presence of Governor Velasquez. This interview was brief and unsatisfactory. Governor Velasquez was an ambitious as well as suspicious man. He had no desire to send young men who had not proven their loyalty to him on adventures which might end in disaster for him. He had already had trouble enough with one Hernando Cortés.

The governor wisely measured Martín López to be

of the same sort as Cortés. He knew exactly how to tame such wild young men. His formula had worked on Cortés. It was simple, indeed—give the young man land to work, an allotment of Indian slaves, let him set up in business, then find him a wife.

"I shall deed you a *repartamiento* of Indians to serve you," the governor said. "You'll have land near the port of Trinidad, a day's voyage along the coast west of here. You'll receive a patent, and the exclusive right to carpenter for that town." Velasquez smiled, adding, "A little later we'll find you a suitable wife."

Martín consented, at least for the moment, to work the land and to set up a carpentry shop in Trinidad. The wife could wait, he decided. There was no hurry.

2 : The Expeditions

Trinidad was a small, flourishing, pleasant town on the south-central coast of Cuba. There was a nice harbor and good lands. With the help of the Mafla brothers and Juan Martinez Narices, Martín set about improving his situation. He developed the land assigned to him, planting it with sugar cane. He had fourteen Indians to work the land. At the same time, he opened a carpentry shop.

Within two years he was doing very well. The Cuban colonies were growing and the villages were spreading out as more and more settlers turned to the profitable sugar industry. New houses were constantly going up and there was a pressing need for doors, windows, chests and furniture.

People in Trinidad thought highly of Don Martín, as they called him. They respected him for his industry and for the fine workmanship of his furniture and other carpentry. There was hardly a house in the town that did not have some example of his work. As a result, he began to live like a young lord. He was able to import fine Spanish wines, beautiful Dutch cloth and brocades.

These comforts hardly pleased him. Carpentry and farming bored him. Trinidad began to weigh heavy upon his spirit. There was little to excite a young man in such a town, for there were no theaters and little other entertainment except an occasional horse race, a cockfight or a fiesta.

The only thing that really interested him was to meet with other young men and talk of the explorations to the west. During his first year in Cuba, the Cordova expedition had brought back astonishing news.

This expedition had set out in February of 1517 to visit the neighboring Bahama islands. Running into a succession of heavy gales, Cordova's three tiny ships were swept westward. After three weeks Cordova found himself on an unknown coast. A landing party was sent ashore. Cordova asked the natives what the name of the country was. The strange Indians replied, "*Tectetan,*" meaning, "I do not understand you." Cordova and his men took this to be the name of the place and they corrupted it into the word *Yucatán.*

Cordova had actually landed at Cape Catouche, the northeastern tip of present-day Mexico's Peninsula of Yucatán.

The men on the expedition were astounded by the

size and solid construction of the stone and mortar buildings they saw—so different from the flimsy bamboo and thatch huts of the Caribbean islanders. The clothing the natives wore, their gold ornaments and their warlike spirit all indicated a higher civilization.

Cordova's small fleet spent several months rounding the peninsula and exploring as far as Campeche before returning to Cuba. Cordova imagined that this new land was an enormous island. He had not thought it wise to try navigating around it, because his company had suffered almost every known peril. Half of the original one hundred and ten men had been lost in the storms and in battles with natives.

Although rumors about rich lands to the west had reached Cuba, until Cordova's voyage there had been no actual knowledge. Now, Governor Velasquez outfitted another expedition of four ships to explore the newly discovered coast. The fleet was put under the command of his nephew, Juan de Grijalva, and it set out May 1, 1518.

News of the new expedition filtered to the center of the island slowly. Martín López first heard of it while seeking hardwoods for his business. He hurried back to Trinidad, hoping the ships might land there and he could join the group. Ironically, Grijalva's ships did stop at Trinidad, but they set sail again a half-day before Martín arrived.

Months passed before anyone on Cuba learned of the fate or successes of Grijalva's men.

Grijalva followed the storm-tossed route of Cordova, but instead of landing at Cape Catouche his ships were driven farther along the coast of Yucatán to the island of Cozumel. From Cozumel the expedition sailed to the mainland and while skirting the rocky coast the men saw what they thought was a mirage: a lonely, gleaming white city on the bluffs facing the sea. It was the sacred Mayan city of Tulum which was to wait long centuries until, in 1842, the famed American explorer Stephens, and his English companion Catherwood, visited it.

The ships sailed around the peninsula, then followed the bowbend of the gulf coast to the beaches of present-day Veracruz. Now and then the expedition touched shore, often meeting with the same unfriendly reception Cordova had experienced. Grijalva, however, was better prepared. His men were well armed, and he carried goods for trading. At one point an Aztec chieftain gave Grijalva many finely worked gold ornaments and other valuable presents.

After six months the fleet returned to Cuba. Grijalva had become the first navigator to open negotiations with the Aztecs. Reports of the expedition's successes blazed across Cuba, flaming through every tiny village. The wildest dreams of every explorer since Columbus now seemed about to become reality. Rather than remaining a cluster of poor islands and jungle-choked coasts, there was promise that the New World held a great and mysterious civilization.

Several of the men who had gone with Grijalva returned to their homes and estates in and around Trinidad. Among them were Pedro de Alvarado, Cristóbal de Olid and Gonzalo de Sandoval, all friends of Martín López. For weeks Martín drove them to distraction. He sought them out at every opportunity, constantly asking them to tell him of their adventures.

Christóbal de Olid, a handsome cavalier with a hawk-like face, narrow hips and the grace of an Arab rider, was also the kindliest. He spent hours telling Martín of the events of the voyage. He spoke of the white city, Tulum, which the natives called Zamá. He recounted the strange tale about Spaniards being held prisoners in that city.

"How can there be Spaniards there?" Martín asked.

"Who knows?" Olid shrugged. "They were not from our company, nor were they from Cordova's. I, for one, do not believe it. We were the first to see that city, but we could not land. The coast is too difficult."

"Well, I shall see the city you speak of," Martín said with fervor.

"Perhaps, or perhaps not," Olid laughed.

"I'm going," Martín replied. "It is said that Governor

Velasquez is planning another expedition to seek the Spaniards who are there."

Olid nodded. "Yes, an expedition is planned," he said. "But it will be made up of men who went on the other voyages. Velasquez needs young men, experienced men, horsemen, cannoneers, men who have learned to fight the Indians. You're too old, Don Martín."

"I'm not yet thirty."

"That is old, my friend."

Martín López' ambition to visit the new shores was more fervid than his good sense, said his neighbors and friends in Trinidad. He was so set on joining the new expedition, he sent his cousin, Juan Martinez Narices to San Jago with a petition to Governor Velasquez. He also began gathering supplies: casava bread, salt pork, rice, clothing and armor. He put his farm and carpentry business up for sale. He had but one thing in mind—the expedition.

At last, Juan Martinez Narices returned from San Jago. The news and message that he brought back were disappointing. The new expedition had been formed. It had set sail from San Jago under the command of Hernando Cortés.

"Cortés' venture cannot succeed," Juan announced. "Cortés set out without the governor's permission, and without the full crew of men. The governor has ordered his arrest for insubordination. A warrant has been sent out that if he puts in at any Cuban port he is to be placed in chains."

The letter for Martín, which Juan Martinez Narices brought back, advised Martín to be loyal to the governor, not to join Cortés, and to stick to his carpentry.

3 : Shipwright Soldier

For days the only thing the people of Trinidad talked about was Cortés' insubordination. Although San Jago was distant, and communications were difficult, every colonist in Cuba had some version of the story.

The closest to the truth was this: excited by Grijalva's and Cordova's reports of riches on the mysterious Mexican mainland, Governor Valasquez decided to send an even larger, better equipped expedition. Being a suspicious and fickle man, instead of entrusting the command to Grijalva, who already had experience and knew the coast, he chose another.

Velasquez picked Hernando Cortés as his new commander, partly because he believed Cortés would be loyal, and partly because Cortés was willing to contribute his small fortune towards the purchase of ships and supplies for the enterprise.

After Cortés had given all his money and had spent weeks gathering men and supplies, Velasquez began. to distrust him. One day a half-witted servant in Velasquez' household, seeing the governor and Cortés strolling in the gardens together, shouted, "Have care, Master Velasquez, or we shall have to go a-hunting some day or other after this same captain of ours."

Although Velasquez appeared to ignore the jester's words, as with all true jests the words influenced him. At the same time, the other men attached to the governor were jealous of Cortés' growing importance. They played on Velasquez' suspicions, deftly turning him against the young captain, until Velasquez finally decided to remove Cortés from the command of the expedition.

Word of this unfair treatment reached Cortés. He acted with the same quick decision which, more than once afterward, would carry him through more perilous situations.

Although he had not completely assembled his complement of men, ships and supplies, Cortés met with his men that very night. He explained his project —the need of sailing immediately. Shortly after midnight, while San Jago was hushed in sleep, Cortés' ships weighed anchor. At dawn the townspeople were astonished to see the fleet slide away from their moorings and head for the open sea.

For a while, the whereabouts of the ill-equipped fleet remained a mystery. In Trinidad, people were split in their opinion as to the right or wrong of Cortés' action. Martín López was among those who stoutly defended the young captain. Although Martín scarcely knew Cortés, something about the man from Medellin appealed to his sense of adventure.

One day, the amazing happened. The small Trinidad harbor seemed miraculously filled with more ships than had ever been seen by the villagers at one time. Martín hurried down to the waterfront and mingled with the excited crowd. The fleet was Cortés'. The young captain had sailed from San Jago to Macaca, stopping there to secure supplies from the royal farms, then had come on to Trinidad to enlist more men.

By noon the town was in a state of gala excitement. Cortés had come ashore. He set up headquarters in one of the houses of a friend and erected his personal standard out in front. The standard, fluttering in the breeze, fascinated Martín López. It was of black velvet, embroidered with gold, and emblazoned with a vivid red cross amidst flames of blue and white. It bore the Latin motto, *Friends, let us follow the Cross; under this sign, if we have faith, we shall conquer.*

This same day, Cortés issued a proclamation inviting men to join the expedition.

Martín López was one of the first to volunteer his services. He was led into the room where Cortés was busily conferring with his lieutenants, who were being sent out into the countryside, to the ranches and haciendas, to buy additional supplies.

Martín was impressed by Cortés' calmness. Nothing in his behavior suggested an outlaw. And yet, this very morning Verdugo, the military commander of Trinidad, had received a dispatch from Governor Velasquez containing orders that Cortés be put in chains if he appeared in Trinidad.

The only reason Cortés was not under arrest at this moment was that he and his lieutenants had boldly walked into Verdugo's headquarters and had told him if he wanted a fight, they would give it. Sensing Cortés' popularity in the town, Verdugo wisely bided his time. He sent a message to Governor Velasquez, asking for reinforcements.

While watching Cortés give orders, Martín judged that the captain was a few years older than himself. In height he was about middle size. His complexion was pale and his large, dark eyes gave him an expression of graveness. Although he was slender, his chest was deep, his shoulders were broad and his frame was muscular.

Cortés dressed in a manner that set off his handsome figure to advantage. He wore a gold chain with a medal on it, and he had a velvet cloak with tassels. Although he gave the impression of being cold and calculating, his speech sounded friendly, even touched with humor.

Having dispatched all of his lieutenants except

Cristóbal de Olid, Cortés turned to Martín and studied him carefully. "If I enlist you in the expedition, Master López, what can you offer?" he asked.

"I offer my sword," Martín replied. "I also have two servants, both able-bodied and strong. And, I can offer three thousand escudos in gold for supplies and equipment."

"I have many swords," said Cortés. "Swords wielded by younger arms than yours. Have you had soldiering experience? Have you fought in the Italian wars?"

"No. I was too young."

"Do you have a horse?"

"No. There is none to be bought. I've tried to purchase one, but as you know, there are few horses on the island."

Cortés nodded, saying, "Olid tells me you have a trade, Master López. We are setting out for a new land. Our purpose is not simply to conquer, but to settle there. Fighting men are useful in securing victories, but they do not always make the best colonists. Men with a trade are needed."

"I don't care to colonize," Martín answered. "It is not my ambition. I have been in a trade long enough. Like you, Master Cortés, I seek something else. Were I anxious to practice my trade, I would have remained in Sevilla."

Cortés and Cristóbal de Olid exchanged glances.

They had already discussed Martín López. Although his fighting ability had never been tested, he could be of help. There were several carpenters among the expedition's roll, but none had the reputation and skills of this man. The ships Cortés had assembled were old, in bad shape and in need of constant repairs. A knowledgeable shipwright could help.

"I'll take you into our company as a shipwright," Cortés offered.

"Do you mean, I must remain with the ship and cannot go inland?"

"What serves a shipwright where there are no ships?"

"Perhaps there is water inland? Or the need to build bridges?"

Cortés smiled again. He admired Martín López' persistence. "Very well," he said. "You can come with us as our shipwright, Master López, whether we are on sea or land."

During the following week Cortés' camp in Trinidad, and the ships in the harbor, were the scene of intense activity. Supplies were brought in from the countryside. More men, including many who had been on the Grijalva voyage, rallied to Cortés' standard. Among these were Cristóbal de Olid, Alonzo de Avila, Gonzalo de Sandoval, Pedro de Alvarado and others, all of whom were to play brilliant parts in the conquest of Mexico. Each time an important cavalier joined up, there were festivities and the firing of salutes from the small brass cannons on the ships.

At the end of the week Martín, accompanied by his servants, the Mafla brothers, and his cousin, Juan Narices, went aboard Cortés' flagship. The fleet sailed from Trinidad to Old Havana where more supplies and recruits were taken on. Here, as at Trinidad, Velasquez' orders to arrest Cortés and his supporters were ignored.

On February 18, 1519, after hearing Mass celebrated by Fray Francisco de Olmeda, the expedition's young, vigorous and level-headed chaplain, the fleet set out upon its great adventure. Nine ships left Havana, and were joined later by three more. The largest of the vessels, the one on which Martín López voyaged, was a one-hundred-ton galleon; three others were in the sixty-ton category; the remainder were smaller caravels and brigantines.

For Martín López, standing on the deck of the flagship, watching the breeze billow the sails of the fleet, it had taken exactly fifteen years since he had first tried to hide aboard a ship bound for the New World to realize his dream of adventure. Now, within the space of two years, he would experience more dangers than most men meet in a lifetime.

4 : Where Is the Spaniard?

Although the ships were ordered to keep as close together as possible, stormy weather soon scattered the fleet. Hurricane winds drove the flagship far to the south so that Cortés and Martín López were among the last to reach the island of Cozumel.

Here, on this pleasing tropical isle, but a half-day's sail from the coast of Yucatán, the expedition laid over, organizing its forces, repairing damage done to the ships and exploring the island. The natives on the island were friendly and the Spaniards were able to visit their curious temples.

One day, Cortés reviewed his forces on the golden beach. The expedition had no more than six hundred and eight men, including one hundred shipmasters, pilots and sailors. The fighting force was made up of five hundred and eight men; thirteen were musketeers, thirty-two were crossbowmen. There were a few bronze cannons and four falconets or very light cannons. Cortés had been able to round up no more than sixteen horses and mares for his cavalry.

Cortés divided his men into companies, assigning the captaincies to his most able lieutenants. Francisco de Montejo, who would later return to Yucatán to conquer and govern the huge territory, was made a squadron leader. Diego de Ordaz, Cristóbal de Olid, Pedro de Alvarado and others received similar commands. Francisco de Orozco, who had fought in the Italian wars, became the chief of artillery. Antón de Alaminos, who had sailed with Grijalva, was the chief pilot for the entire fleet.

Martín López had to be content with the role of chief shipwright. Although he resented what he considered to be an unromantic task, he worked hard putting the ships back into shape. At times he chafed at not being allowed to go along with the groups exploring the island, and he suspected that Cortés thought him too old for such rigorous activities.

In actuality, Martín, Cortés, and one or two others were the old men of the expedition. The majority were in their early twenties, some were in their teens. The youngest of the future *conquistadores*, as the world would eventually call them, was a lively, fair-haired boy of fourteen named José Ortega. He served as Cortés' messenger and page boy. He was a favorite of all the men, and everyone called him "Orteguillo," meaning "Little Ortega."

During the weeks that it took for the daring expedi-

Atlantic Ocean

Gulf of Mexico

CUBA

Villa Rica de la Cruz

Vera cruz

Santiago

AZTECS

QUETZALCOATL

YUCATAN

Mexico Tlascala Tabasco

Pacific Ocean

tion to cross a hurricane-tortured sea from Cuba to Yucatán, then to coast clockwise around the Mexican rim of the Gulf, Martín saw sights that fired his imagination. He was happy he had come on the voyage in any capacity.

Of all the early adventures, there were two which most amazed him. One was the rescue of a man named Jerónimo de Aguilar; the other was the rescue of an abandoned dog.

At Cozumel the expedition definitely learned that two Spaniards were held captive on the mainland. A ransom of beads and other goods was sent through native traders in the hope of releasing the men.

One morning while Martín López was working on a ship with his friend Hernán Martín, a blacksmith from Havana, he saw an Indian boat approach the beach. The two men, along with Melchorejo, went down to the water's edge. Melchorejo was a native of Yucatán. He had been captured by Grijalva and had been brought back to Cuba where he learned Spanish. He was now the expedition's translator.

Melchorejo became very excited. "It is the prisoner, the Spanish prisoner," he told Martín.

As far as Martín López could make out, there was no Spaniard among the people who piled out of the pirogue. "Where is the Spaniard?" he asked.

"The one with the golden sandal," replied Melchorejo.

Martín was still puzzled. The man with the golden sandal looked no different than the natives who accompanied him. He was middle height, dark of skin, and his hair was long, cut like the hair of the other Indians. He wore one gold sandal and had the other tied to his belt. He wore a ragged cloak of an Indian-woven cotton and a loincloth.

The man was a Spaniard, indeed. But he had lived among the Indians so long, he had come to look like them. At first he had difficulty speaking for he had almost forgotten Spanish.

When Martín López led the party to Cortés' quarters the Indians crouched outside the door of the thatched hut, and the man squatted exactly as they did. When Cortés appeared, his reaction was the same as Martín's. He wanted to know where the Spaniard was.

The squatting man squinted at him and said, "I am the Spaniard. I am Jerónimo de Aguilar."

Reaching for Spanish words that he had almost forgotten, Aguilar haltingly told his story. He was a native of Ecija, in Spain, where he had studied for the priesthood. He had come to the New World as a missionary and had gone to serve in Darien, which is now Panama. The tiny colony failed, so Aguilar and fifteen companions has set sail for the Carribee islands. Their ship had been caught in a storm and wrecked. Clinging to an overturned small boat, Aguilar and a handful of companions had been washed ashore near Tulum. The five surviving men had been captured by natives.

"Except for one other companion named Gonzalo Guerrero, the others were sacrificed on the Indian altars," he explained. "I was made a slave in the household of a chieftain in the white city that lies down the coast. Because I worked hard and could be trusted, the chief made me his household majordomo."

"What happened to the other man—Guerrero?" Cortés asked.

"He is alive, but would not come."

"Would he rather remain a captive among the barbarians?" Cortés asked, surprised.

"No. He is no longer a captive," replied Aguilar. "When I was set free I went to the place where he lives. He refused to come with me. He said, 'Brother

Aguilar, I am married to a native woman and I have three sons. The Indians look upon me as a captain in wartime. Leave me be. My face is tattooed and my ears are pierced. What would the Spaniards say if they saw me? I have the appearance of a savage.' "

Cortés sent young Orteguillo to get a doublet, a cloak and others garments for Aguilar. He would soon value the man greatly. Although Aguilar had not been allowed to travel freely, nevertheless he knew a great deal about the Indian life and customs. And, most important, he spoke Mayan, the language of Yucatán and Campeche.

The other rescue which so delighted Martín López had to do with a dog, an animal that would one day save his life.

Martín had gone with the pilot, Escobar, on a reconnaissance trip far ahead of the fleet. They went with a dozen men in a small, swift, shallow-draft vessel, following the coast past the Bay of Campeche to a large natural harbor called the Laguna de Terminos.

When their small ship probed into the tremendous harbor, a brilliant new world opened before Martín's eyes. Although Cuba and the Yucatán coastline had their palm trees and tropical verdure, much that he had seen was dry and brushy. It had been only a little more exotic than the bleakness of his native Spain.

The Laguna de Terminos was like nothing he had ever seen before.

The curving shoreline, ringing the vast mirror of water, was like a vivid green frame of luxuriant foilage, brilliant flowers, great mangrove swamps, jungle plants flapping wet feelers in a faintly stirring breeze. The streams emptying into the lagoon were like glistening tunnels hollowed through the massive verdure. As the ship glided closer inshore, Martín could hear the whining call of catbirds, the strident squawking of parrots, and the deep, monotonous sound of the countless insects in this mysterious world.

For hundreds of miles behind this barrier of jungle lay a region of lagoons, swamps and meandering rivers —the haunts of flamingos, wild ducks, peccaries and spotted jaguars. The shoreline seemed utterly deserted, as though no human had ever lived in the region.

While the men observed the shore with fascination, suddenly an animal leaped from the jungle and raced gracefully along the sandy beach, following the route of the boat.

"Dog! A dog!" cried the lookout.

"It looks like an Andalusian hound," someone else said.

A small boat was put down. Martín, along with a half-dozen men, rowed ashore. Curiously, instead of exhibiting fear or a growling caution, the dog rushed up to the boat as it beached. It leaped about, wagging its tail and making other signs of welcome.

"It is an Andalusian greyhound," Martín said with wonderment.

The greyhound, a female, allowed him to pet her. She leaped up, licking his face, behaving as if he were her long-lost master. Then, as the men explored along the beach, searching for springs of fresh water, the hound ran alongside, tail wagging happily.

When Martín returned to the brigantine he brought the dog aboard. The pilot, Escobar, who had been on the Grijalva voyage the previous year, recognized the animal. "She was on one of Grijalva's ships," he said. "I remember that a dog was left behind."

Evidently, the greyhound had thrived in the New World, despite the jaguars, serpents and other perils. She had grown fat, but was lonely.

"I would like to keep the dog as my own," Martín told Escobar. "In Andalusia we have a proverb—Lose a dog, lose your luck; find a dog, and find good luck."

5 : The Horse Gods

The first long halt made by Cortés' expedition on Mexican soil was at the Grijalva River, which the Spaniards then called the Tabasco. Although the purpose of the stop was to trade with the Indians, it was there Martín López first showed his skill with the sword.

Dangerous reefs at the mouth of the river prevented the galleons and brigantines from entering, so one afternoon, Cortés' men rowed upstream in small boats. As they glided up the jungle-bordered river, Martín López, acting as lookout in one of the lead boats, soon noticed that armed natives were dodging back and forth behind the dark mangrove trees along the banks. He flashed word back to Cortés.

That night the men camped on an island in the river. In the morning they saw that the opposite shore was crowded with warriors. Undaunted, the Spaniards headed across the river. Through Jerónimo de Aguilar and Melchorejo they tried to get permission to land. The Indian reply was an abrupt attack. Canoes lanced out from the shore. A flight of arrows hissed overhead. Then both sides grappled fiercely. Martín López' small boat overturned and he found himself struggling in waist-deep water with a copper-skinned warrior.

Martín cut the man down with a slash of his sword, then turned upon another attacker. The Spanish and Indian war cries, the clash of Spanish steel and native obsidian, echoed over the river. Slowly, the Spanish forced the Tabascans to the riverbank. There, the Spaniards were able to form ranks and open fire with their crossbows and arabesques.

Stunned by the sound of the arabesques, the first guns they had ever heard, the Tabascan warriors fled in panic. The Spaniards pursued them and, in a short time, took possession of their chief town—the first sizable town captured in Mexico by the *conquistadores*. However, although the Indians had lost this first battle and had abandoned their town, they still had not given up.

That night the Spaniards camped in the courtyard of the principal temple.

Shortly before dawn, while on guard duty at an outpost beyond the temple, Martín López was disturbed by an unusual rustling sound. He called out a challenge. There was no answer. With his sword unsheathed he crept forward until something swinging from a tree branch brushed his shoulder. He leaped to

one side, made a deadly parry with his sword. Still nothing stirred.

Finally, in the dim light, he made out the object that so disturbed him. Some Spanish garments dangled from a tree. He pulled them down, then called another sentry to take over while he took the clothes to Cortés' headquarters.

By the light of a small fire Martín, Pedro de Alvarado and Cortés examined the garments. They were the clothes which had been worn by the native interpreter, Melchorejo.

"He's been murdered," Alvarado said. "The Indians must have slipped in and killed him."

"But we would have found his body," said Martín.

A search was quickly made of the camp. Neither a living, nor a dead, Melchorejo could be found. It was finally decided that Melchorejo, homesick for his own people, had abandoned the Spanish camp. He had undoubtedly left his European-style clothing behind because, if found in them, he might have been killed by his own countrymen.

Though the loss of Melchorejo as an interpreter was not important, since Jerónimo de Aguilar could translate from the Mayan just as well, the flight of the Indian could still be dangerous. Up to now the Indians imagined that the Spaniards were white gods. It was feared that Melchorejo would inform his people how few men Cortés had in his party, and that they were ordinary humans, not deities.

The impact of this was felt later in the day, and on the next, when thousands of Indians from the great deltalike region massed near the town, and the little band of Spaniards was engaged in several desperate battles. The overwhelming Tabascan forces were actually defeated by Spanish cannons and cavalry. The Indians were surprised and terrified by the flash and roar of the cannons, and by their first sight of men mounted on horses. They imagined that horse and rider were one—a strange, fearful kind of god.

After the battles, when the Indian chieftains came to make peace and pay tribute to Cortés, Martín López was deeply impressed by Cortés' cleverness and brilliant strategy.

Cortés had noticed the Indians' terror of the horses. In the New World there were no large domestic animals such as horses or cattle. Almost the only domestic animal was a small, edible dog. The largest and most feared of the wild animals in Mexico was the deadly jaguar. Just before the meeting with the Indians, Cortés ordered Juan Sedeño's mare, which had given birth to a colt aboard ship the day before, to be brought ashore. The mare was hidden in some thickets a short distance upwind from where Cortés waited for the Indians.

At noon forty Indian chiefs arrived. They wore richly embroidered mantles and headdresses made of vivid quetzal feathers. They saluted and perfumed the Spaniards with incense, as was their custom.

With Aguilar interpreting, Cortés scolded them for having waged war. He told them that if they caused any more trouble the *tepuzques*—the cannons—would jump out and kill them.

At this instant a signal was given to an artilleryman hiding in the brush a short distance away. He fired a loaded cannon. The thunder of the gun and the crash of the cannonball through the trees awed the Tabascans.

Before they fully recovered from their fright, another signal was given and one of the Spanish stallions was led to a place not far from where the Indians stood. The horse, getting wind of the mare hidden in the brush, began to neigh and snort, to paw the ground and to rear up in a violent manner. The Indians imagined that the stallion's wild behavior and apparent anger was directed at them. They stood frozen with terror.

Cortés finally ordered Alvarado to take the stallion away. He told the Tabascans that he had ordered the horse not to be angry at them as long as they remained friendly and peaceful. This strategy made such an impression on the Indian chieftains, who believed the horses were gods and the Spanish could direct them, that they readily agreed to become subjects of the King of Spain and to obey Cortés' every command. The next day they brought more gifts for the Spaniards, including twenty daughters of nobles.

Among these girls who were given to the Spaniards to act as servants and prepare their food was one called Malintzin. The Spaniards had trouble with her name and corrupted it into Malinche. She and the other girls were baptized Christians.

Before long this girl would become as important in the success of the conquest as either Cortés or Martín López. She was a girl of unusual beauty, character and intelligence. Malinche was not a Tabascan. She had been born at Painalla, on the southeast borders of the Aztec empire. Her father was an important chieftain. After his death, and in order to deprive her of her inheritance, Malinche's mother sold the girl to some traders who carried her to Tabasco.

It was through Malinche that the Spaniards learned of the importance of a certain giant ceiba or cotton-wood tree in the nearby Tabascan town of Zintla. The tree was honored in the pagan rites of the people. Thus, before leaving Tabasco, Cortés ordered Martín López to go to Zintla and carve a huge Christian cross in the tree. When it was seen that Martín was not struck dead by the Indian gods, the people marveled.

Even today, because of Martín's cross, the Indians of Christian Mexico look upon the ceiba tree as sacred, and they will not cut one down.

6 : The Aztecs

Leaving the Tabascan region, Cortés' fleet continued northward along the Mexican coast. A steady breeze filled the sails and the ships hugged the shore so closely inhabitants could be seen on the beaches all along the way.

The explorers were feeling good. They had been refreshed by their stay in Tabasco. They were in high spirits because of their victories over the Indians. They looked forward to new adventures. Almost all of the men had forgotten the threats of Governor Velasquez in Cuba.

During these pleasant days aboard ship Martín López was fascinated by the Tabascan slave-girls who accompanied the expedition. He was especially interested in the girl Malinche. He was touched by the fugitive tenderness of her dark eyes, and by her pleasant personality. Frequently, Martín and the page boy, Orteguilla, spent hours on the deck trying to converse with the girl. They had already begun to learn Mayan words, but at times they were quite puzzled when she spoke another strange tongue which she called "*Ná-huatl.*" It sounded completely different than Mayan.

After less than a week's voyage the fleet came to the island of San Juan de Ulua, which Grijalvo had named the year before. The ships anchored on the leeward side of the island, hardly a stone's throw from the mainland.

Soon Indian canoes and pirogues or war-boats came out to meet the Spanish vessels. The Indians were friendly. They boarded the ships, bringing gifts of fruit and brilliant flowers. When Cortés tried to talk with the leaders, both he and Jerónimo de Aguilar were baffled, for these people spoke a tongue that was completely strange.

During the attempts at conversation, Martín López discovered that some of the words these Indians used were similar to those he had learned from Malinche. He informed Cortés of the girl's knowledge of this strange language. Malinche was sent for. Thus, by a roundabout method, with Malinche translating what the Indians said into the Mayan tongue, then Aguilar translating it into Spanish, Cortés was able to converse with the Aztecs.

For the next few months, while in the land of the Aztecs, Malinche and Aguilar would work as a team, interpreting for the expedition. It would not be long, however, before Malinche learned Spanish and could translate directly. Likewise, several of the Spaniards, especially Orteguilla and Martín López, soon learned to speak *Náhuatl*, the language of the Aztecs and most of the people in central Mexico.

The day after anchoring near San Juan de Ulua the Spaniards moved their camp to the sand dunes on the mainland. They put up shacks and placed their cannons in defensive positions. There was no need for caution, however. The Indians were curious and friendly. For a while the Spanish camp resembled a fair. The Indians flocked in from great distances to trade food and ornaments of gold for the colored beads the Spaniards offered.

The natives of the coast told the Spaniards stories about the Aztec Confederation, a powerful empire that controlled much of the country. They spoke of the great Aztec city, Tenochtitlán, which lay in a beautiful mountain valley almost two hundred miles inland. They spoke of the power and magnificence of the Aztec emperor, Moctezuma.

At first, Martín López and his companions only half believed these accounts. It was hard to imagine a civilization so advanced, so rich, so powerful, existing for so many centuries without the whole world knowing about it. But doubts quickly changed. Within a short time the Spanish camp received several official visits from the Aztec governor of the region and from ambassadors sent down from the Aztec capital.

The visits of the ambassadors were most impressive. The first ambassador brought royal gifts which included loads of finely woven cottons, beautiful capes made of iridescent hummingbird feathers, numerous wicker baskets filled with ceremonial ornaments made of beaten gold.

The second embassy was even more awe-inspiring. It was led by two Aztec nobles from Tenochtitlán who were accompanied by one hundred slaves. The ambassadors wore richly embroidered robes and breechcloths. Each bore a crooked golden staff and carried roses. The natives of the region treated them like gods and knelt before them.

The ambassadors brought stunning gifts from Moctezuma, the emperor. These were richer than the first ceremonial gifts. There were shields, helmets, bracelets and collars of pure gold; robes of exquisite workmanship; and vessels of silver. Among the gifts were two large disks the size of cartwheels: one, made of pure gold, represented the sun; the other, of silver, represented the moon.

Although the Spaniards did not guess the meaning and significance between the first and second group of gifts, they were awestruck by their opulence. Here, at last, were the treasures they had endured hardships to seek.

The wealth of the Aztecs and the apparent size of their empire was beyond anything Martín López had ever dreamed of. It inspired him with a burning curiosity to see their wondrous capital. Some of his companions, however, began to have fears and doubts. Could so small a band of explorers safely enter the Aztec heartland, especially after Moctezuma's second ambassador had announced the rich gifts were for the King of Spain, and that the Spaniards should now leave the country?

In the great city of Tenochtitlán—where Mexico City now stands—reports of the arrival of strange, bearded men on the Mexican coast caused untold excitement. The Aztecs asked, "Who are these strangers—gods or men?"

Although the so-called Aztec empire had reached its zenith of greatness at this time, certain religious omens caused fear and uneasiness in their barbaric world. According to an Indian legend, some centuries before the arrival of the Spaniards an important hero-god of an earlier civilization, the Toltecs, had been driven from Mexico by his enemies. This god, Quetzal-coatl, also called the Plumed Serpent, was the deity of the winds, the patron of culture, and the symbol of life. Some believed he was a man who had become a god. It was said that he had a fair complexion and a flowing beard—characteristics which few Indians had.

From one end of Mexico to the other, people believed that when Quetzalcoatl had been driven from his domain by enemies, he had sailed across the Atlantic Ocean to a mysterious place called Tlapallam. Before leaving, he had prophesied that he would return someday and, messiah-like, take possession of the country.

During Moctezuma's reign various ominous signs were seen which foretold the return of Quetzalcoatl and the end of the Aztec empire. One omen had been the strange agitation and flooding-over of Lake Texcoco which damaged many houses in Tenochtitlán. There had been no heavy rains, no earthquake nor storms to cause this phenomenon.

A year later one of the towers of the principal temple in the city took fire without cause. For days afterward, no matter what was done, the fire could not be put out. Shortly afterward, three comets were seen in the sky; a sure sign of Quetzalcoatl's approach. Finally, just before the Spaniards arrived, a strange light spread in the eastern sky, forming a flaming pyramid. The light was accompanied by weird wailing and voices from the sky.

When the Spaniards landed on the coast, carrying

sticks that belched thunder and lightning, riding awesome beasts, it was feared that Quetzalcoatl, or at least his lieutenants, had returned. Did these strangers not have pale complexions and beards like the deity? Did they not come in vessels mysteriously driven by the winds?

Anxious rumors raced across the land like wildfire. When news of the Spanish landings was brought to Moctezuma's court, the emperor was filled with dismay and apprehension. He consulted with his counselors and high priests.

Some of his lords felt that the Spaniards should be driven back into the sea. Others, believing the strangers were gods, said nothing could be done. The priests announced that the omens were about to be fulfilled. Some said that the only way to ward off doom was to wrench thousands of living hearts from the breasts of victims in their barbaric human sacrifices. If the Aztec gods were offered enough blood, they might help.

Moctezuma was uncertain. Torn by this and that advice, he was unable to act. He did not know whether he should welcome the visitors or fight them.

Fearing that the Spaniards might be allied with Quetzalcoatl, he first sent gifts to Cortés that were of unusual royal and religious significance—gifts to please the gods.

After his emissaries returned to Tenochtitlán with reports about the Spaniards, and especially pictures they had made of them, Moctezuma suspected they might be mere men rather than gods. His second load of gifts, the shields, golden helmets, the great gold and silver disks, were a kind of bribe to hasten the withdrawal of the visitors from the country.

The gifts, of course, had the opposite effect. They stirred the Spanish imagination and quickened the desire of the explorers to see Moctezuma's fabulous capital.

Cortés had no intention of leaving. He had already sent scouting expeditions up the coast to locate a better campsite. The new base, a short distance up the coast, was built as a permanent settlement, and was called *Villa Rica de Vera Cruz* (Rich Town of the True Cross).

While establishing their coastal base, the Spaniards made friends with the Totonac Indians, who were an unwilling ally of the Aztecs. Martín López, Cortés and his lieutenants frequently visited in the Totonac city of Cempoalla, which was ruled over by a tremendously fat man whom they called the Fat Chief. They learned much about the Aztec world from the Totonacs.

Moctezuma's empire was not as happily united as the Aztec ambassadors had boasted. It was full of cracks. Mexico was like the Hellenic world at the beginning of Rome's greatness. It was made up of numerous city-states and tribal civilizations who were under the domination of the warlike Aztecs. Although these smaller city-states paid tribute to the Aztecs, many of them—the Totonacs, for example—feared and hated the Aztecs.

Some of the tribute-paying nations were ready to join forces with any powerful knight who might wage war against the Aztecs. Others, though they were allies of Moctezuma, would just as soon sit back and watch the fighting.

This situation gave Cortés and most of his men a feeling of confidence. They saw the possibility of inserting a wedge within the cracks in the Aztec confederation and bringing the whole structure down. However, before Cortés could attempt any such strategy, some accounts had to be settled in the Spanish camp.

Certain of the men who had come on the expedition, especially friends and followers of Governor Velasquez, wanted no part of an invasion into the Aztec heartland. Some were frightened by the enormous risks. They had already seen the bloody human sacrifices of the Aztecs. They were afraid to penetrate so mysterious a land, inhabited by millions of Indians, protected by huge armies.

One night some of these men seized a brigantine and prepared to set off for Cuba to report to Governor Velasquez. The plot was discovered. At midnight Cortés sent a party aboard the ship and arrested the men.

Then, to discourage any further ideas of escaping, Cortés did a most dramatic thing. He sent Martín López and Juan de Escalante, along with some sailors, to remove all the gear from the Spanish ships. They carried ashore the cordage, the sails, cables, anchors, and all the removable metal parts.

"Everything of value has been taken off," Martín reported to Cortés.

"Now beach the ships," Cortés ordered. "Beach them and set fire to them."

The entire Spanish camp gathered on the beach, their eyes fixed on the awesome sight. Martín was aware, as he watched the flames destroy the fleet, that many of his companions were crying. It was a terrible feeling to stand on the beach of an inhospitable country and burn your only means of escape. Many of the men despaired of ever again seeing their families in Cuba and Spain.

Now, there could be no retreat from adventure.

7 : To the Valley of Decision

It was the middle of August, 1519. Martín López could look back on the past five months and be amazed that so much had been done. He and his comrades had sailed uncharted seas, had explored a coast, fought battles with Indians, set the foundations for a city, and had burned their bridges behind them. All these accomplishments were but a preparation.

Now the time was at hand for the greatest adventure of all—scaling the mountain heights of central Mexico and breaching the Aztec fortress.

In the middle of March, leaving a small party to guard Villa Rica, the Spanish expedition set out on its incredible trek toward Tenochtitlán, Moctezuma's capital. The men were pleased to be on the move once more.

A few of the older, less headstrong men like Martín, were eager, but thoughtful. They could dwell on the risks. He realized how great the odds were against success, even against survival. Only a handful of his companions were trained soldiers experienced in warfare and, least of all, Indian warfare. How could a few hundred men, a dozen or so horses, and the small Spanish arsenal of guns challenge a whole civilization that numbered millions of people?

In spite of the grim picture that rose before his eyes, Martín was confident. Like his companions, he was passionately religious. He believed that when he fought for his faith, God would protect and advance his cause. Although the *conquistadores* were indeed greedy for gold and riches, in their complex personalities there was also a real and sincere belief that they must convert the Indians to Christianity.

Martín also had a deep confidence in the leadership of Cortés. He had already witnessed examples of Cortés clever generalship, courage, and ability to turn the most difficult situations to his benefit.

Instead of marching directly toward Moctezuma's capital, the Spaniards headed toward Tlaxcala, a small, proudly independent nation almost surrounded by the Aztecs. The Tlaxcalans were a rugged people. They were incredible fighters. They were bitter enemies of Moctezuma. Martín López knew that if the Tlaxcalans could be won over as allies, it would be a useful step.

Leaving the coast, the little army marched in good order. Scouts went out ahead and along the flanks.

Most of the cavalry were in the lead, followed by half the foot soldiers, then came the baggage and supplies, carried by Totonac allies. The rearguard included more foot soldiers, bowmen and some horsemen. During each day's march, and while camping at night, a constant vigilance was maintained.

The route Cortés chose went from Cempoalla toward Xalapa, an Indian town where the present-day city of Jalapa stands; then to Socochima, which opened upon the interior highlands.

Accustomed to the arid landscape of Andalusia, the richness of Mexico offered new surprises for the Spaniards. The verdure seemed to change, as did the climate, with each day's march. After leaving the area of burning sand dunes and brush, the men slowly climbed through country that was intoxicatingly lovely; a world of humid mists, forests smelling of vanilla blossoms, trees filled with exotic flowers and brilliant birds.

The trail took them up to the great Mexican tableland, about six thousand feet above the sea. The air here was clearer and more invigorating. The scenery became grand, even frightening, as the awed explorers went around the bases of mighty peaks that gleamed at night with volcanic fires, and glimmered in the day with snowy mantles.

During the first stages of the march the men stopped

at friendly villages allied with the Totonacs. Then they halted for three days at a large Aztec town where they were received with coolness. Fortunately, the chieftain there had gotten no instructions from Moctezuma, who still couldn't make up his mind what to do about the visitors.

At last, the expedition entered Tlaxcalan country. It was a region of rich forests and cool-running streams.

Although Cortés had sent word ahead, asking permission to enter the country and arrange an alliance, Tlaxcalan friendship was not easy to gain. Surrounded as they were by deadly enemies, the people of Tlaxcala were suspicious. Their friendship had to be gained the hard way—in battle.

Before the Spanish marched very far into this region they met armed resistance. One day they awoke to find themselves confronted by an enormous Tlaxcalan army of some fifty thousand warriors. When Martín López saw them his heart sank. This was no army of indolent Tabascan natives. The Tlaxcalan warriors were handsome and tough. Their army was organized in good formations. They wore brilliant outfits and carried lances, longer than Spanish lances, as well as fearful-looking, obsidian-edged battle axes and swords. They came at the Spaniards with insignias and banners flying.

The two sides clashed with fury. Martín López felt

the Tlaxcalans were the most daring and formidable fighters he had ever faced. Several times during this first battle it seemed as though the entire Spanish company would be crushed. It was a miracle when the Tlaxcalans withdrew from the field.

A few days later another battle was fought, as furious as the first. In it the Spaniards suffered so severely that hardly a man escaped receiving some wound. As in Tabasco, the turning point was when Spanish guns and crossbowmen opened fire. The deadliness of these weapons, as well as the startling effect the Spanish horses had on the Tlaxcalans, finally convinced the latter to sue for peace.

The news of the Spanish victories over the Tlaxcalans spread rapidly throughout Mexico. It astonished the Aztecs and their allies. Again they wondered, were these strangers men or gods? How had so small a force vanquished the undefeated Tlaxcalans? Many were sure, now, that the omen predicting the triumphal return of Quetzalcoatl was coming true.

Even the Tlaxcalans who had fought against and had wounded Spaniards believed there was something godlike and invincible about these strangers. When they sent their peace delegation to the Spanish camp one of their leaders approached, placed one palm on the earth, kissed it, then bowed three times as though he were addressing the figure of a god in a temple.

The chieftain announced that the people of Tlaxcala placed themselves under Cortés' friendship.

To keep the Indians believing his men were more than ordinary mortals, Cortés wisely held back for several days before marching into the Tlaxcalan capital, thus giving his little army time to treat the wounded, repair armor and put on a good face. When they finally entered the city of Tlaxcala, Martín López was amazed by the welcome given by people who had fought so bitterly just a few days before.

The streets and flat-roofed houses were crowded with smiling men, women and children who threw flowers at the conquerors. They quartered the Spaniards in the finest houses. For days afterward there were endless rounds of celebrations and banquets.

During the twenty days that Martín was in Tlaxcala he spent much of his time wandering around the city and strolling into the surrounding countryside. Being a carpenter more than a soldier, wherever he went, whether it was along the placid river that flows through Tlaxcala, or into the oak and pine forests, he could not help but make a mental note of the fine timber he saw. His memory for the Tlaxcalan hardwoods and how they might be floated on the river would eventually become a key in the conquest of Mexico.

Early in September the expedition set out once more

for the Aztec capital. Martín López had made so many friends among the Tlaxcalans, he found it hard to leave them. They, in turn, were worried. They warned the Spaniards of Aztec treacheries, and they even sent a large corps of warriors to accompany the Spaniards.

The warnings had not been idly given. After leaving Tlaxcala, the expedition narrowly escaped several ambushes by Aztec allies. By now each man had learned the need of constant alertness; of never being without his armor, awake or asleep; of keeping the horses saddled even at night; of having the guns, cannons and crossbows always loaded.

Their vigilance paid off. Finally, after struggling from the sea coast to the eight-thousand-foot high central plateau, the Spaniards found themselves near the gateway of the Aztec stronghold.

During this time Moctezuma remained uncertain and unable to act. His few attempts to bribe the Spaniards into departing, his disastrous attempts at having them ambushed, had all failed. It was as if the mysterious, bearded visitors had all-seeing eyes; as if they knew exactly where to expect trouble, and how to ward it off.

About the first week in November of 1519 the Spanish covered the last lap of their journey. They moved rather slowly because, in addition to their own numbers, more than a thousand Tlaxcalan warriors accompanied them.

The route wound through picturesque country until, at length, the narrow road climbed up the bold sierras separating Mexico's mile-and-a-half-high valley from the surrounding regions. The road narrowed to a path as it scaled through the pass between two of the highest peaks on the North American continent—the snow-covered volcanoes, Popocatepetl and Iztaccíhuatl.

Martín López was in the advance scouting group that first crossed the twelve-thousand-foot-high pass. As he staggered over the rocky ground, panting for breath in the rarefied air, the piercing winds blasting down from the icy mountainsides numbed him to the bone.

Suddenly, upon turning an angle in the trail, he forgot all the hardships and discomforts. Before him, in the distance, lay one of the most breathtaking sights in the world, the Valley of Mexico or Vale of Anahuac.

In the brilliant visibility of the noonday sun, almost a mile and a half above sea level, he could look down upon more level terrain in an unbroken unit than he had seen all the way up from the coast. Here was Mexico's most populous valley; shimmering stretches of noble forests, lakes, fields of golden maize and blue-

green maguey intermingled with orchards and bloom-
ing gardens.

In the center of the great basin, rimmed by towering
mountains, were the lakes—the Aztec seas. The borders
of the various lakes were rimmed with towns and ham-
lets while, in the midst of the largest lake, lay the
jewel-like Aztec capital, Tenochtitlán. From the
heights of the mountain pass the fair city, with its
white towers, pyramid temples, palaces, hanging
gardens of flowers and its countless canals, was inviting
and beautiful. The city appeared larger than any city
Martín had ever seen in Europe, and, indeed, it was.
When Martín gazed down upon this Venice of Mexico,
it was a city already two centuries old. It possessed
over sixty thousand houses, and a population of more
than three hundred thousand.

As the various units of Cortés expedition pushed up
into the pass, each man was struck with the same feeling of wonder that Martín had experienced. But while
many of the men excitedly gazed down upon the rich
prize, thinking of the gold and loot lying there,
Martín's thoughts turned in another direction. He saw
in that valley evidences of a civilization and a power
far superior to anything he had expected to find there.

Although he did not know it yet, more than a
million and a half people lived in the valley. Here was
gathered all the political and military might of the

Aztecs. It was, he thought, the valley of decision. Whoever controlled the Vale of Anahuac, controlled all of Mexico. Could a few hundred battle-scarred Spaniards and a thousand or more Indian allies dare enter the valley and live to tell the tale?

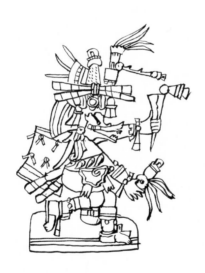

8 : Tenochtitlán

I t took two days for the expedition to worm its way
down the difficult trail from the high pass between
the volcanoes to the perpetual springtime of the valley
floor. While going down, some of Martín's companions
wanted to turn back. They feared entering so populous
a region. Some suspected a trap. They argued with
Cortés that they should go back to Villa Rica and wait
there until a much larger Spanish force was assembled
to conquer the country.

They were quite right in suspecting a trap. In
Tenochtitlán, many of Moctezuma's advisers who had
argued for an all-out war against the Spanish now
changed their tactics. They had decided that it was
wiser to invite the small Spanish force into their capital. In this manner it would be easier to cut the Spaniards off from their base, easier to keep them from
enlisting new allies and, in time, they could destroy
them. Tenochtitlán would be the trap.

Cortés understood this danger. Nevertheless, like
most of his men, he was moved by curiosity and ex-

70

cited by the opulent prize that lay within reach. And, like most Spaniards of that day, he was fearless. Martín López sided with Cortés. As he said, "We are here at last, why not go in?" But he was also a practical man. He believed in analyzing the dangers that lay ahead, and planning for them.

While en route down into the valley Martín frequently paused to study the great basin and its complex of lakes. There was something about the lakes and the causeways connecting the island-city to the surrounding shores that troubled him.

There were six interconnected lakes in the valley. The largest was Lake Texcoco, a broad, shallow inland sea. To the south of it, connected to it by canals and channels, were two smaller lakes named Chalco and Xochimilco. These smaller lakes were slightly higher than Texcoco, their waters being held back by dams and causeways. To the north of the great pivotal lake lay another group of smaller lakes—San Cristóbal, Xaltocan and Zumpango.

Tenochtitlán, the capital city, stood on islands in the northern part of Lake Texcoco. To reach the city from the mainland one had to cross the lake over one of the four causeways which stretched across the water like great wheel-spokes. One of the causeways was narrow, the others were like broad avenues, wide enough for eight horsemen to ride abreast. The principal causeway extended southward from Tenochtitlán, seven miles across the water to the lakeside towns of Mexicaltzingo and Iztapalapa. In the middle of the lake a narrow, spur-causeway branched off from this main lake-avenue to the village of Coyoacan. The other important causeways linking the city to the northern and western shores of the lake were called the Tepeyac and the Tacuba causeways.

Along these lake-spanning avenues there were numerous bridges so that the water could flow freely from one part of the lake to the others, and so Indian canoes could pass easily from one area to another. At various points on the causeways, especially at the bridges, there were towers and other fortifications which made the approaches to Tenochtitlán quite impregnable.

Somewhat to the east of Tenochtitlán, and not connected to the city, was a great dike, stretching more than ten miles from north to south, which divided the lake into two unequal halves. This dike had numerous sluices which let water through from one side to the other, but which could be shut during periods of flood to protect Tenochtitlán from inundations. It was called the Netzahualcóyotl Dike after the noted poet, engineer and ruler of the city-state of Texcoco which lay on the eastern edge of the lake.

During one of the rest stops, while coming down

from the pass, Pedro de Alvarado found Martín López frowning at the distant lakes and causeways. "What are you looking at, Master López?" Alvarado asked.

"The water, Don Pedro. The water."

"Yes, it's a fine sight. Such beautiful lakes. You know, when I was in Spain, a mere boy, I dreamed of owning a small lake of fresh, sweet water."

"I fear the lakes," Martín replied.

Alavarado laughed. "But why? You will not have to swim them."

"There is just too much water for us, when we have no ships."

"That is just the talk of a shipwright," said Alvarado. "You look at a body of water and you want to build a ship. Well, Master López, wait until we've conquered this land. You'll be able to build ships to your heart's content."

The next day Martín's worries about the lakes left his mind, nudged aside by the vivid experiences of entering the greatest city in the New World.

The Spaniards had slept in a palace in the lakeside town of Iztapalapa, then had set out at dawn across the causeway to Tenochtitlán. Throughout the morning, just as on the previous day, they were followed by hordes of curious people eager to get glimpses of them. Thousands of canoes paddled in from nearby villages, skimming along both flanks of the causeway. Most of the boats were small, quick-gliding vessels capable of holding three or four men; others were huge pirogues or war canoes large enough to accommodate fifty warriors.

At a point on the causeway called Acachinanco, where there were elaborate fortifications, and where the Coyoacan causeway joined the principal causeway, several hundred of Moctezuma's chieftains waited to welcome Cortés.

The Aztec nobles were dressed with barbaric splendor. They wore finely woven cotton *maxtlatl* or loincloths, flowing capes which were brilliantly colored and embroidered. On their necks and arms they displayed collars and bracelets of turquoise mosaic. Their ears, noses and underlips, which were pierced, were decorated with pendants of jade or small gold crescents.

Through Jerónimo de Aguilar and Malinche, the chieftains conferred with Cortés, then led the Spanish expedition on to the gates of the city. There, at a bridge, they waited for Moctezuma's retinue to arrive. After a little while the glittering cortege appeared.

Indian officials bearing the gold wands of authority appeared first. Then the royal palanquin, carried on the shoulders of nobles, moved toward the bridge. The palanquin was shaded by a canopy of burnished gold, vivid feathers and sparkling jewels. The train stopped.

The palanquin was lowered and Moctezuma stepped out from beneath the golden canopy. Mats of embroidered cotton were laid upon the ground for him to walk upon. He was accompanied by the lords of Texcoco, of Iztapalapa and other cities.

Martín López pressed forward in the crowd to get a glimpse of this man who was so feared and revered.

Moctezuma wore a girdle about his waist that was decorated with gold. His cape, made of embroidered cotton, was embellished with countless pearls. His feet were shod with sandals of pure gold. He wore a headdress of green quetzal feathers, an emblem of military power.

Martín thought the Indian monarch might be seven or eight years older than himself. Moctezuma was of average height, well formed, not too thin nor fat. He was quite handsome, and carried himself with a grave and dignified air.

There was a ceremonial exchange of gifts and a brief conference between Cortés and Moctezuma. Then the monarch retired to the city while his brother led the Spaniards into the city and to the huge palace of Axayacatl which had belonged to Moctezuma's father.

This was the evening of November 8, 1519—a memorable date in the history of the world.

On this first day Martín López and his comrades had very little chance to see the Aztec city in any detail. They were like diplomats or tourists being whisked directly into a fancy hotel. They had spent the entire day crossing the lake, and in ceremonies with the Aztecs. What they saw of the fabulous metropolis was limited. As they proceeded to the palace, the streets were crowded with thousands of men and women. It was somewhat like their entry into Tlaxcala, but with one notable difference—no one showered them with flowers. When they reached the Axayacatl Palace, in the very center of the city, everyone was dead tired. Still, there was no time for rest. They had to set up guard posts, locate their cannons at advantageous points and arrange their quarters.

During the early evening, the men not on duty wandered about in the palace, exploring its vast chain of rooms and patios. The palace was extraordinary. It was so extensive there was ample room for the entire Spanish company, their horses, and the thousand or more Tlaxcalans who had come with Cortés.

The building was low and thick-walled, almost like a fortress. It consisted of one story, except in the center where there was a second floor. The various apartments were of great size and were separated from each other by immense courtyards with fountains and gardens. The best apartments were decorated with flowers, with gay cotton draperies, and the floors were covered with woven mats. The beds were made of thick, springy mats made of woven palm leaves. They had coverlets of cotton.

Later that evening Cortés ordered all the cannons to be fired. It was done partly to celebrate their arrival in the city and, even more, to impress the Aztecs. The thunder of the guns, reverberating in the city, shaking the foundations of houses, the acrid stench of powder floating through the streets, reminded the people of the eruptions of their volcanoes, and it filled their superstitious minds with dismay.

The night was a strange one for the people of Tenochtitlán. Here in their midst, at last, were the strangers. Were they gods? Had they come to destroy? The echo of the iron-shod feet of the Spanish horses on the city's pavements must have disturbed their sleep. What fearful animals! And what strange garments the Spaniards wore—garments of steel glistening in the sun. And worst, these strangers had brought with them the ancient deadly enemies, the Tlaxcalans.

For the Spaniards, too, it was a most unique night. They were bedded down in a palace more luxurious than the palaces of the kings of Spain. Here they slept in the midst of a gaudy, barbaric civilization, thousands of miles from their own homeland. If help were needed, none would come. They were here, alone. No one in Cuba or Spain knew where they camped this night.

Martín López took his turn at guard duty after midnight. The strange city was silent. A sliver of moon hung above it like a pale silver scythe. From the second-story roof of the palace he could see the somber shapes of the great pyramid temples, and beyond them, the glimmer of the lake. The lake was something that menaced him.

9 : The Lake Brigantines

For several days the Spaniards were under orders not to leave the palace. No one knew exactly what was going on, except that Cortés, some of his lieutenants and Moctezuma had had several meetings. One morning, while walking his greyhound in the palace gardens, Martín met Cristóbal de Olid, who was very close to Cortés.

"What is happening?" he asked Olid impatiently. "We've suffered much, we've risked much to get here. Now, do we have a plan? It seems to me we have nothing in mind but loose ambitions—to convert these heathens to Christianity and to make them vassals to our king. But how do we go about it?"

"We don't have a plan, yet," Olid replied.

"So, what shall we do? Just sit?"

Olid shook his head. "Cortés has decided there is no need to plan any operation until we know more about these people. We must learn more about their ways of thinking, their defenses and their cities. Then it will be time to act."

"And how is that done, always sitting here in this palace on battle alert?"

"The sitting is over, Master López. Today we shall begin exploring the city. Each day an armed party will go out to look at a different section of the city."

Gradually, and always with caution, the Spaniards began to familiarize themselves with the Aztec capital. It was no easy task. The city was large and complex. During such sorties Martín was impressed by the great network of canals running in every direction through the city. There were as many canals as there were broad avenues or narrow streets. One could actually penetrate every corner of the city by canoe. Martín was quick to see that anyone who wanted to control the capital had to control the canals and bridges.

One day the Spaniards received permission to visit the chief temple or *teocalli*, which was less than a block away from their palace. The party, led by Cortés, also included Martín López, Gonzalo de Sandoval, Juan Velasquez de León and a dozen soldiers.

The huge pyramid was built in a series of stages. On its level top stood the sacrificial altars and the temples dedicated to the Aztec Rain God, and to the squat, diabolical Huitzilopochtli, the God of War. The shrines themselves were like charnel houses, smelling of blood and incense, their walls covered with smoke. The sight of them sickened Martín.

Here, and in other temples dotting the city, some twenty to fifty thousand human beings—slaves and warriors captured in battle—were sacrificed yearly. The prisoners were stretched, face up, upon a jasper sacrificial altar. Their arms and legs were secured by priests who wore long black robes and whose hair and clothing were matted by dried blood. A chief priest plowed open the victim's chest with a razor-sharp obsidian knife, then would plunge his hand into the opening and wrench out the living heart. This he burned, while it was still throbbing, in a carved stone vase. The smoking hearts were placed at the feet of a figure of the god within the temple building.

The Aztecs believed that their gods required such sacrifices, otherwise the world would come to an end. But more gruesome still were the evidences Martín saw of the ceremonial banquets held after a sacrifice. Though the Aztecs were not primitive cannibals who ate human flesh to satisfy hunger, their religion demanded a ritualistic eating of human flesh. Following a sacrifice, the body of the victim was given to the noble or warrior who had captured him. The warrior was required to serve an elaborate banquet, with lavishly prepared dishes and beverages. The principal ceremonial dish included the cooked flesh of the victim.

During the sacrifices a huge war drum, its head

covered with skins of large snakes, was beaten. The dismal sound could be heard more than five miles away.

A day or two after the visit to the *teocalli*, Martín saw the great market at Tlaltelolco in the northern section of the city. It consisted of a vast square of polished pavement, bordered by arcades which sheltered many of the merchants. It reminded Martín of tales he had heard of the famed Persian bazaars. He had never in his life seen so many things for sale in any one place.

Each kind of product, gathered in from the Aztec empire, was displayed in its special place. One section was completely devoted to vegetables which were arranged in symmetrical heaps on woven mats. In another section cotton goods were sold. Elsewhere was a row of venders of implements and tools; obsidian knives, burnished pottery, spindle whorls, copper axes and needles. The booths of the feather salesmen were like rainbows. Some sold merely bunches of plumes; the green of the quetzal, the multicolored plumage of parrots. At other stands feather cloaks, feather mats and feather-decorated shields were displayed.

Day after day Martín and his companions saw new marvels, all of which impressed them with the might and richness of the Aztec lords. On a number of occasions they visited Moctezuma's own palace, a red building across the broad central plaza from the Spanish quarters. The palace was filled with courtyards and fountains. The apartments were immense, having ceilings of elaborately carved, sweet-scented wood, walls hung with richly dyed drapes and skins of wild animals. It was like the palace of an oriental potentate, and Moctezuma himself lived on a similar scale.

Martín had heard that the monarch had over one thousand wives and was surrounded by countless nobles who personally served him. When the highest chieftains of the land came to confer with him, they put aside their fancy garments and approached him barefoot, their eyes humbly turned to the ground, never once looking at him. This they did because they believed he was directly descended from the gods.

One day Martín was involved in the uncovering of Moctezuma's treasure, which marked the beginning of real trouble between the Aztecs and their guests. A companion of Martín, a carpenter named Yañez, noticed that a section of one of the walls in their quarters had recently been plastered over. Egged on by curiosity, the two men removed the new plaster. They uncovered a passage that led into a large, musty room.

Lighting torches, they investigated. It took but a moment to discover they had found a fabulous treasure vault. They were stunned by what they saw: bars of gold and silver, fanciful gold ornaments, figures of jeweled animals and birds, all done with the most exquisite workmanship.

Martín stood guard over the treasure while Yañez ran to tell Juan Velasquez de León, Cortés' chief lieutenant. A few minutes later Juan Velasquez and Cortés came to see the treasures.

"This is the treasure of Moctezuma's father," Cortés finally explained. "Malinche has spoken of rumors about it. For the moment, I entrust you men to keep this secret. We shall seal up the wall, and we shall say nothing to anyone."

Although the men kept their secret, it did no good. Certain Aztec servants had seen what had happened. Moctezuma was informed, although he said and did nothing about it. However, other Aztec nobles were told. They felt that since Moctezuma did not punish the Spaniards, it was a sign of weakness. Even though the monarch was believed to be a descendant of gods, they began to talk of revolting against him and overthrowing the Spaniards.

Cortés had no way of determining how serious the danger was. But he sensed trouble and he refused to be caught napping. His first move was to get Moctezuma to come for a visit in the Spanish quarters. When the monarch arrived, he was told that he was a prisoner-hostage. Although he was held as a prisoner,

Moctezuma let his people believe that he was staying with the Spaniards of his own choice. Why the Indian monarch did this remains a mystery. He may have had some secret plan of his own, or, it may have been cowardice that motivated him. He may have even tried to bribe the Spaniards into releasing him, for during this period he turned over the treasure to Cortés.

Sensing the mood of the people, the Spaniards were also becoming nervous. Martín López, Cristóbal de Olid and Juan Velasquez de León repeatedly warned Cortés that the city was a trap. With removable bridges on the causeways, and the causeways so narrow it was impossible for fighting men and cavalry to maneuver on them, there was no way for the Spaniards and their Tlaxcalan allies to retreat if an attack came.

Cortés understood this quite clearly. Finally he ordered Martín López to construct some ships. "Make us vessels, Master López," he said. "Make them large enough to transport all our Spanish companions and all our horses and cannons across the lake. Do it with all speed."

Some of the Spaniards were dubious about the ships. They felt the decision came too late. How could four brigantines be built in time? It remained for Martín López to accomplish the impossible. He had already drawn plans for ships capable of navigating the shallow waters of the lake. He had even made a survey of all the Spaniards and had found fifteen men with skills useful in shipbuilding. There were carpenters, blacksmiths and sailmakers.

His principal helpers were his carpenter-servants, the Mafla brothers, his cousin, Juan Martinez Narices, a master sawyer named Diego Hernandez, and also Andrés Nuñez who had been a shipwright in Spain.

Runners were sent down to Villa Rica, on the coast, with orders that enough gear, sails, iron and rope from the destroyed fleet be sent up to Tenochtitlán to outfit four brigantines. Meanwhile, Martín and his staff risked their lives, going out some ten miles from Tenochtitlán to an area of rich oak forests in order to cut the necessary timbers for the ships.

To keep Moctezuma's enemies from attacking, Cortés again employed one of his clever ruses. Playing on the Aztecs' superstitious beliefs concerning Quetzalcoatl, the God of the Winds, Cortés let it be known that these would be the vessels of Quetzalcoatl, who would make them move without the use of oars or paddles. The curiosity of Moctezuma and his enemies was so great, they waited to see the marvelous ships.

On the bank of a canal that passed beside the Axayacatl Palace, work in Martín's makeshift shipyard went on day and night. The workmen sweated under the Mexican midday sun; they toiled by torchlight in the chilly Mexican nights. In just a little over three months the four brigantines were completed, tested and launched.

Each ship measured about twenty-seven cubits, that is, thirty-nine feet in length. To navigate in shallow waters, they were broad-beamed and shallow-draft. Each vessel had a well-deck to accommodate oarsmen and seamen. There was also a raised rear poop, and a raised foredeck on which brass cannons were mounted. Although the ships could be propelled by oars, Martín was counting on their tall masts and square-rigged sails to spread wonder among the Aztecs.

One day, when a fair wind blew across the lake, the ships were tested out. They caused an enormous sensation among the Aztecs, who had never seen vessels of such size and stateliness. But it was the mysterious principle of the sail and the rudder which so awed the people of Tenochtitlán. When the sails of the brigantines filled with wind, billowing white against the blue Mexican sky, and the ships raced across the water, maneuvering with ease, the people imagined the god Quetzalcoatl had something to do with them.

10 : Danger from the Sea

Although Hernando Cortés was always friendly toward Martín López, respecting him for his sound outlook and his courage, Cortés had often seemed amused that a Sevillian carpenter should seek adventure. Now, as a result of the swift shipbuilding job, the leader of the expedition regarded Martín in a new light. Martín had handled his men so well, Cortés was highly impressed. He began to feel that Martín was as important to the success of their venture as his other lieutenants.

When the ships were launched, he called Martín into his apartment and told the shipwright that he was giving him a new commission.

"To command the brigantines?" Martín asked. Having worked so hard on the ships, he had set his heart on being the navigator and commander of the tiny fleet.

"It is not command of the fleet," Cortés replied. "It is a far more important task, and a dangerous one. As you well know, the Aztecs would attack us at any moment, but for one thing."

"What is that?"

"Moctezuma. The Aztec king is still revered. He still has the power to hold back the impetuous chieftains. If he were to believe that we plan to remain in Mexico forever, or that he would always be our prisoner, I think he would give his people a signal to war on us. But he believes we might leave. I have told him we shall go."

"Then we retreat?" Martín asked.

Cortés smiled, but his dark eyes were as hard as obsidian. "We shall soon withdraw from the city," he said. "But not from Mexico. Our curiosity led us into a den of tigers. It will soon be time for us to leave the den and establish a base where we can rally the Indian nations as our allies, then return and crush Tenochtitlán. However, we have to play for more time. I have told Moctezuma that we are building ships on the coast so that we can leave his country. I want you to take your men, go to Villa Rica, and build us a ship. It should be a large caravel."

"But why build it if we do not leave?" Martín asked, puzzled.

"You must be seen working on a ship. You will certainly be followed by Aztec spies. Furthermore, we shall require the ship. When we leave Tenochtitlán we'll take the treasure with us. The ship will carry it to the king in Spain," Cortés said.

Thus, hardly giving his artisans a moment's rest, Martín called them together, ordering them to be ready to march within an hour.

The small group, without more military protection than their own swords and lances, made the long journey to the coast in five days. Arriving at Villa Rica they celebrated a happy reunion with friends who had remained there guarding the fort. Martín conferred with Gonzalo de Sandoval who had recently come down to Villa Rica from Tenochtitlán to command the fort. Sandoval assigned a number of men to help on the shipbuilding.

Wasting no time, Martín laid out a makeshift shipyard on the coast near the mouth of the Cempoalla River. Since there was no suitable lumber along the coast, he made trips a great distance inland to the forest slopes of the towering Orizaba volcano, in order to cut ship timbers. The trimmed logs were floated down the Cempoalla River to the coast.

The caravel, a large ocean-sailing vessel, soon took shape. The timbers for the keel and hull were formed. Rodrigo de Nájera, one of Martín's most skilled men, set up the sternpost and bow. Each man did his tasks well, but the speed with which the whole operation was done must be credited to Martín López. Cortés had judged the man well. Martín had shown himself to be more than a capable shipbuilder. He was a fearless leader and organizer. He inspired his men so that they worked without fear in dangerous country far from the main body of Spanish soldiery. He also commanded the respect of the Fat Chieftain of Cempoalla, who sent him hundreds of Indian workers to help cut timbers and raise the ship's scaffolding.

While the caravel was being built by the sea, in Tenochtitlán the lake brigantines continued to exert the psychological effect on the people that Cortés had hoped for. During several months the swift, well-armed vessels ranged over the lake, sails billowing majestically. They performed two important functions. They continued to awe the Aztecs who believed the God of the Winds moved and protected them. On the practical side, Cortés used the ships to carefully explore the entire shoreline of the Aztec sea, the inlets, the villages and the fortifications along the various causeways leading to the capital.

Fascinated by the sight of "the winged ships," as the Aztecs called them, Moctezuma asked Cortés if he could voyage aboard one of them. Cortés readily granted this wish. He realized it would give the prisoner-ruler prestige in the eyes of his people, and it would help put off the feared revolt of the nobles.

A rich canopy was fixed upon the poop deck of the best ship. Royal rugs were laid upon the deck. Moctezuma and a handful of his loyal chieftains boarded the *capitana* or principal brig. The monarch's son and other lords were taken on the other brigantines. Juan Velasquez de León, Cortés' captain of the guard, Pedro de Alvarado, Cristóbal de Olid and Alonzo de Avila were in command of the ships and the two hundred Spanish soldiers and sailors who went on the trip. Several hundred of Moctezuma's fastest war canoes accompanied the brigantines.

The ships set out for a rocky island in the lake, a sacred isle upon which only the Aztec monarch and a few of his high priests were ever allowed to set foot. Cortés had carefully chosen the hour for this excursion. Usually, in midafternoon, a fresh breeze blew up across the lake. The desired breeze rose, the sails filled and, to the astonishment of Moctezuma and his retinue, the brigantines scudded over the water without a man touching an oar. Within a few minutes the fastest of the native war canoes had been left far behind.

According to Bernal Díaz, the chronicler of the conquest, the swiftness of the vessels delighted Moctezuma. The monarch had seen no horses until the arrival of the Spaniards, and his people had no vehicles or means of locomotion that moved any faster than

their own feet or canoes. It was no wonder that Moctezuma, sailing smoothly aboard the brigantines, imagined he was being borne on the wings of gods.

While the brigantines exerted their magic upon the
imaginations of the Aztecs, Cortés, pleased by the reports he received concerning Martín López' successful
operations on the coast, had the audacity to send out
small groups of his men to explore distant regions. At
times a single Spaniard went out, accompanied by
Indian guides. They searched for gold mines and began making alliances with outlying communities.

Occasionally news of these forays reached Martín
López' camp. A young soldier called Pizarro, who was
not yet twenty, traveled to the northern frontiers of
the Aztec empire. Another of Martín's friends, the
thin-bearded Diego de Ordaz, made a forty-day journey through unknown country to the Coatzacoalcos
River.

Despite this seeming freedom to move about in a
hostile country, the Spanish in Tenochtitlán were not
sitting easily. The magic spell of the lake brigantines
began to wear off. Twice, making use of Moctezuma's
power, Cortés had to nip hostile plots on the part of
certain Indian chieftains. The men in Tenochtitlán
lived in a continual state of semi-siege.

One day in April, almost six months after the Spanish had entered Tenochtitlán, trouble finally came. But

instead of being the expected Indian insurrection, the trouble came from the sea. On that day Martín's Andalusian greyhound was playing on the sandy beach not far from the shipyard. The faithful dog, which had journeyed back and forth across Mexico with his master, suddenly began barking at something in the sea. Since the shipyard workers could see nothing unusual, they paid little attention to the dog's warning. Often, the animal caught sight of dolphins in the water and went wild with excitement.

The dog kept up her insistent barking for several hours. Finally, Martín sent a man down the beach to investigate. When the man returned he was as excited as the dog.

"Master López!" he shouted breathlessly. "Master López, there is no need to build the ship. Ships have come. I see a great fleet of ships approaching the coast!"

Martín ran down to the beach. Indeed, there were ships. In the distance, on the cloud-flecked blue horizon, he saw a fleet of galleons and caravels much larger than the fleet in which he and Cortés had arrived on this shore. He immediately sent a man to the fortress-settlement of Villa Rica to warn Gonzalo de Sandoval.

11 : Battle With Narvaez

The host of lordly Spanish galleons, caravels, swift brigantines and smaller vessels was definitely a threat to Cortés' little band of adventurers. The commander of the approaching fleet carried orders to arrest Cortés and his men, to put them in chains and transport them back to Cuba for trial.

The unexpected threat, coming at a moment when Cortés could least afford to be troubled with arguments with his own countrymen, had been ordered by Governor Velasquez of Cuba.

At the time that Cortés had burned his own fleet on the beach before marching on Tenochtitlán, he had dispatched a small boat to Spain. The vessel, commanded by Montejo and Puertocarrero, had been commissioned to carry Cortés' report of his discoveries in Mexico, as well as Moctezuma's gifts, to the king in Spain.

Unfortunately, the ship paused at the tiny Cuban port of San Lucar before going on to Spain. Word quickly spread across Cuba of the marvelous discoveries in the world to the west. Details soon reached the ears of Governor Velasquez. Already jealous of Cortés' successes, and feeling all this newly discovered world belonged to him, Velasquez assembled a huge force to pursue and arrest Cortés.

The governor outfitted eighteen ships. He enlisted over nine hundred men; eighty of them cavalry, eighty who were arquebusiers, one hundred and fifty crossbowmen and much heavy artillery. His army was supplied with large quantities of ammunition and other military stores. He also sent a thousand Cuban Indians to act as bearers and servants.

This imposing expedition, many times the size, and far better equipped than Cortés' group, was commanded by the Castilian *hidalgo*, Pánfilo de Narvaez, Governor Velasquez' most trusted lieutenant. Narvaez was the arrogant, self-important man who had once laughed at Martín López' ambition to serve the governor as a soldier.

Although Governor Velasquez had some grounds for dissatisfaction with Cortés, he had no right to arrest him. While the new expedition was being outfitted in Cuba, the Spanish king had decided it was foolhardy for Spaniards to fight each other. Either they should join forces for the conquest of Mexico, or they should be kept apart. The king sent orders to Velasquez and Narvaez, commanding them not to bother Cortés, and to do their exploring in some other area. Disobeying the king's wish, Pánfilo Narvaez set sail for Mexico.

When his fleet dropped anchor not far from Martín López' shipyard, Narvaez established a camp ashore and proclaimed his intention of marching against Cortés' men. Being overconfident, he expected little trouble. He knew that Cortés' forces were thinly spread out—the main body in Tenochtitlán, Martín López' small group at the shipyard, and Sandoval with a handful of men at Villa Rica. He could take on each group separately and defeat them at will. Thus, instead of marching against Villa Rica with a suitable force, he simply sent several men there to demand Sandoval's surrender.

Martín López had already dropped everything he was doing at the shipyard and had marched with his small group to Villa Rica in order to help defend the settlement. The two men were good friends and worked well together.

Although Sandoval was ten years younger than Martín, the latter greatly admired the brown-bearded, husky young lieutenant. Sandoval was the sort in whom courage and good judgment were combined. Although he stammered, he was a good officer. He looked after his men and they, in turn, were willing to follow him anywhere.

When Narvaez' men rapped on the wooden gate

at Villa Rica, arrogantly demanding the surrender of the settlement, Sandoval had some Indian helpers throw net hammocks over the intruders, making them prisoners. Narvaez' chagrined emissaries were tied up in the nets and were sent on the backs of Indian runners, in relays, all the way to Tenochtitlán. For the prisoners, the four-day trip, by this novel mode of travel, was certainly most harrowing.

After the prisoners were delivered to Cortés, he ordered them set free, then in his skillful way, he won them over to his cause. He learned from these men that Narvaez, despite the size of his expedition, was losing support. The man's arrogant, bullying manner irritated many of his followers.

Playing for time, Cortés sent the released prisoners back to Narvaez' camp. He supplied them with gifts of gold for themselves, and more presents to distribute to their friends. At the same time, he sent his chaplain, Father Olmeda, to negotiate with Narvaez.

A few days later, leaving Pedro de Alvarado with a garrison of two hundred men in Tenochtitlán, Cortés set out with the remainder of his force for the inevitable showdown with Narvaez. In six days he arrived at Villa Rica.

Meanwhile, Narvaez had landed all his troops and had captured the Totonac city of Cempoalla. He held the Fat Chieftain and other allies of Cortés as hostages, and he made Cempoalla his headquarters. He sat there, complacently believing that Cortés, Sandoval and Martín López, with their loyal but small army of two hundred and fifty men, would sooner or later come to their senses. There was nothing they could do against nine hundred well-armed men but surrender.

Cortés had been counting on the arrival of some two thousand Indian reinforcements, warriors of the Chinateca people, who were noted for their skill with an exceptionally long war lance. When the Chinatecas failed to appear, he decided to risk battle against Narvaez without them.

On the evening of May 27, 1520, Cortés' weary, battle-scarred company approached Cempoalla. In the late evening the exhausted men slept beside a rain-swollen stream while Martín López went out ahead to scout.

Having been in the area so much, Martín knew the region as well as the palm of his own hand. Working his way through the coastal brush, his movements hidden by the complete darkness, by the rushing of wind and the sound of intermittent rain, he finally located Narvaez' battle-camp. Narvaez had posted the bulk of his army in a field about one quarter of a mile from the Totonac city.

While cautiously scouting the area, trying to locate the exact position of the enemy pickets and artillery,

Martín noted a curious tumult in the enemy camp. At first he imagined Narvaez had learned that Cortés' men were nearby. It seemed as if Narvaez' army was marching out to attack. Then he was puzzled; they were heading in the wrong direction. Finally, he realized that the men were marching back to Cempoalla. Narvaez' troops, unaccustomed to hardships, battle and the idea of continual vigilance, were distressed by the rain. They were returning to Cempoalla where there was shelter.

Martín hurried back to his own camp and reported to Cortés. The men were quickly aroused. They checked their armaments, ate a quick, cold meal, drank from the muddy stream, then formed up in march order. A squad of scouts, led by Martín, set out first. In a drenching rain that allowed little visibility, they forded the angry river. The few artillery pieces were then brought across.

The little army moved in silence. For once they went without the usual fanfare of fifes and drums which they had always used to impress Indian enemies. Although ready to fight, many of the men did not expect to see the dawning of the next day. The odds against them, once again, seemed impossible. They prayed and hoped for luck. For some of the men, especially Cortés, Sandoval and Martín López, there was no choice but to fight, and if necessary, to die fighting. Narvaez had offered a prize of two thousand pesos to whoever should kill any of the three.

At midnight they came to the edge of the town. The men on foot slipped through the streets like shadows until they had almost reached the plaza facing the principal pyramid temple. A Mexican dog barked, alerting the encamped enemy. Cortés and his dozen horsemen, waiting at the edge of town, now raced in.

The battle began in total darkness. Narvaez' men fired their guns and crossbows from the doorways of the houses they had slept in. Frequently they fired at fireflies, taking them to be the flare of matches from Cortés' muskets. During the fighting it rained intermittently; at one moment the black sky opened in a drenching downpour, a moment later clouds parted briefly and the city was bathed in a cold steely light.

Cortés and his horsemen moved swiftly about the town, attacking wherever they were needed. Meanwhile, Sandoval and Martín López led an attack up the steep steps of the pyramid, intent on gaining its flat crown where Narvaez had his headquarters within the thatched-roof temple building.

For a short while it appeared as if Narvaez' men would hold the temple heights. The stone walls of the building protected them, and they could fire effectively whenever one of Sandoval's men showed his head above the top step of the pyramid.

It was now that Martín López settled an old argument with Narvaez, and also won lasting fame in the eyes of his companions. With sword in one hand and a flaming torch in the other, Martín leaped to the crest of the pyramid, raced across its flat deck and set fire to the roof of the temple building. As the flames quickly spread through the tinder-dry underlayer of thatch, the defenders within the building were smoked out.

Martín lunged at them, slashing left and right as they ran from the entranceway. During the fray he wounded Narvaez. Within seconds, Sandoval and his men had joined him and they soon disarmed Narvaez and his followers.

The midnight battle had taken less than two hours. It not only brought victory to Cortés, who had defeated an army three times the size of his own, but it also changed his position. He was no longer a hunted man. He was now the supreme leader of the Spaniards in Mexico, and he enjoyed the support of his king.

When dawn came, Cortés dealt out justice. He released the Fat Chieftain and his nobles who had been imprisoned by Narvaez. He sent Narvaez and some of his commanders to Villa Rica, to be held there in chains. He prevailed on the rest of Narvaez' men to join his own force. He sent Martín López off to dismantle Narvaez' ships and bring all the gear ashore.

He also made plans to enlist more Indian allies to help him capture Tenochtitlán.

Unfortunately, Cortés and his men had little time to enjoy the pleasures of their victory, or to properly organize their campaign against the Aztecs. When Martín returned to Cempoalla after having dismantled the ships, he found the Spanish camp busily packing, and Cortés in an angry mood.

"There is a revolt in Tenochtitlán," Cortés said. "They're attacking Alvarado. They've burned your brigantines, Master López."

12 : Escape

"**W**e march on Tenochtitlán at once," Cortés announced.

Absorbing Narvaez' soldiers into his own force, Cortés now had an army of about twelve hundred men. There were a hundred musketeers, almost a hundred crossbowmen, and nearly a hundred horses. Leaving a small group behind to guard Villa Rica, the expanded army traveled in swift, forced marches toward Tlaxcala and Tenochtitlán.

On June 24, 1520, having covered the two-hundred-mile route up from the coast, the rescue army reached the long southern causeway leading into the Aztec capital. This time the native welcome was far different from their first welcome. No gaudy array of Indian nobles came to meet them. Near the edge of the city, in the shallow, reed-thick waters, Martín López spied the burned hulks of the four brigantines he had built.

Upon entering the city, Martín and his companions felt chilled by the atmosphere of animosity that lay upon the city like a pall of silence. Tenochtitlán appeared deserted. As the army marched through the streets the ring of horses' hoofs upon the pavement was answered by a melancholy echo.

The men who had been in the city before dreaded the silence. They feared that Alvarado's small garrison had met with disaster. Finally, as they approached the gates of Axayacatl Palace, they heard a shout of joy from atop its walls. Alvarado's men lived!

After the first moments of happy reunion within the palace, Cortés and his lieutenants turned to the serious business of taking stock of their situation. The Aztec revolt had been triggered by the rash actions of Pedro de Alvarado. While Cortés was away dealing with Narvaez, the young, headstrong lieutenant began to suspect that the Aztecs were planning to attack his garrison during one of their religious festivals. During the fiesta he had made a bold attack on the people while they were celebrating a religious dance. His cruel slaughter of the innocent dancers enraged the people of the city.

For many days the garrison was under siege. Provisions and powder had dwindled. Not too many of the defenders had died or were injured. Malinche, the page boy Orteguilla and Moctezuma were safe. However, the garrison suffered severely from lack of water. Instead of assaulting the palace and taking it by force, the Aztecs had decided to starve its occupants.

The day after Cortés brought in his new army, the Aztecs decided to renew the assault. Indian forces numbering more than one hundred thousand warriors began furious daily attacks on the palace. The Spaniards struck back, sending out flying squadrons in an attempt to break through the Indian encirclement and secure a passageway to the causeways leading across the lake.

The fighting raged day and night. The palace walls belched forth an unrelenting sheet of flame and smoke. The groans of the wounded were lost in the thunder of artillery and musketry, in the hiss of arrows and the wild battle cries of the massed Indian population.

At night, when the battle sounds diminished, the Aztecs tortured the Spaniards by shouting, hour after hour, "The gods have delivered you into our hands at last. The War God, Huitzilopochtli, thirsts for blood. The stone sacrificial altar is ready. The knives are sharpened."

When Spaniards fell into the hands of the Indians, their companions defending the palace witnessed the horrifying ritual on the nearby pyramid. They saw their companions stretched, belly up, upon the altar. They saw the flashing obsidian knife plunge down into the chests of friends who fought, slept and adventured together. During such moments, Martín López felt that the bloody knife was ripping into his own chest.

To relieve the intense pressure, Cortés decided to use Moctezuma's authority. He hoped that an appearance of the monarch might restrain the fury of the people. Either by force or guile, he made Moctezuma mount to the roof of the palace. The monarch wore his imperial robes: the *tilmatli* of white and blue, his royal gems, his golden sandals and the imperial feathered headdress.

Surrounded by several nobles and a guard of Spaniards, Moctezuma strode along the parapet of the palace. He was recognized by the crowds below. Abruptly, the war cries and din of arms ceased. A deathlike stillness spread throughout the area. Aztec warriors who had been assaulting the palace a moment before prostrated themselves in the streets.

Moctezuma's features were weary and sullen. He gave a pained smile. He was like a man suffering a secret illness, rotting quietly. In a melancholy voice he told his people they should stop fighting. "The Spaniards are my friends," he said. "I am not their prisoner. Now, I command. Open a passage for them to leave our city and our land."

When the monarch said he was a friend of the detested invaders, a murmur of contempt rippled through the crowd. "Traitorous Aztec!" someone cried out.

The cry multiplied, became a swell of anger. A shower of arrows and stones descended on the spot where Moctezuma stood. It had come so suddenly the Spanish guards were unable to protect the monarch. Moctezuma fell, seriously injured by a rock. He was carried back into the palace where he died within a few days—a bitter, rejected lord of a great empire.

Moctezuma's death unleashed the total fury of the entire Aztec world upon the besieged Spaniards.

Cortés held a meeting with his lieutenants. It was clear that they could hold out but a few more days. They must make a desperate break for freedom. During the war council Pedro de Alvarado advised that they try to reach the Tacuba causeway.

"It is the shortest of the escape routes," he argued. "Once we reach the mainland we can circle around the northern rim of the lake toward Tlaxcala. It is the area that is least populated."

"Cannot the burned brigantines be raised?" Cristóbal de Olid asked.

Cortés shook his head. "The hulls are sunk in the marshes."

The war council settled for the Tacuba escape plan. They discussed the preparations and reconnaissances that had to be made. Then Cortés called Martín López in.

"I have an idea for a weapon which will help us open a passage to the causeway," Cortés explained. "We require a cover or shield that will make us impervious to the Indian arrows. You must engineer these weapons for us, Master López."

The weapons suggested by Cortés, and constructed by Martín López and his artisans, were a kind of mobile war tank—the first tanks used in the New World. These tanks or *mantas*, as they were called, consisted of a frame of beams armored with heavy planks. They had two chambers, one above the other, which housed musketeers who fired their guns through loopholes in the front and along the sides. The tanks were on rollers and could be maneuvered by manpower.

The Aztecs were astonished and momentarily paralyzed when they first saw these rolling fortresses rumbling through their streets, belching smoke and fire. With the *mantas* the Spaniards were able to explore their escape route, to clear and patrol certain streets beyond the palace.

Plans were made for a general retreat. For several days and nights Martín López and his men worked without rest, constructing a large, portable bridge which would be taken along to span gaps in the causeway. Men prepared their weapons; baggage was packed; the Aztec treasure was divided among the men, except for the portion destined for the King of Spain.

At midnight, July 1, 1520, the gates of the palace were swung back. Silently, the Spaniards and their

Tlaxcalan allies filed through the gateway into the drizzling rain that blanketed the city. The lead column, made up of twenty horsemen and two hundred infantry, was led by Gonzalo de Sandoval and Diego de Ordaz. The "battle" or center, which included the baggage, the treasure, the heavy guns, was commanded by Cortés. Malinche, as well as a number of important Aztec hostages, including two of Moctezuma's daughters, traveled in this group. The rearguard, made up of horsemen and the bulk of the infantry, was led by Pedro de Alvarado, Martín López and Velasquez de León.

The long train wound through deserted streets without trouble until it reached the causeway. Here Martín supervised the swinging of the portable bridge over the gap where the city street ended and the causeway began. Just as the bridge was laid, Aztec sentinels raised an alarm.

Suddenly, almost as though the entire city had awaited this signal, a bedlam of sounds broke forth. Priests on the temples began beating the deep-throated, dismal drums. The sounds of conch horns could be heard. These were followed by the approaching, strident cries of warriors.

Martín López waited in the darkness at the bridge, watching the Spanish column cross. He greeted friends as they passed—Olid, Yañez, his cousin, Juan Martinez

Narices, Orteguilla and Fray Olmeda. When the last of the long column had gone by he ordered his crew to raise the bridge and drag it onto the causeway so it could be taken ahead to span the next gap.

Now, disaster struck—the first of the night's many horrors.

Pedro de Mafla, at the far side of the bridge, shouted to Martín, "The bridge is stuck. We can't move it."

Martín hurried across the span to investigate. What he saw filled him with dismay. The weight of all the horses, the heavy cannons, the baggage, and the trampling of so many feet had wedged the bridge timbers firmly into the muck and stones. The bridge could not be raised.

He ordered his men to abandon the work, to hurry across and join the Spanish column. They had hardly joined the rearguard when an ominous, gathering sound was heard. It was like a mighty forest agitated by winds. The sound grew louder and louder. Then, the men heard the splashing of paddles.

Suddenly, as if by magic, thousands of Indian canoes appeared through the drizzle on each side of the causeway. The canoes skimmed across the dark waters of the lake and dashed against the sloping stone sides of the causeway. Shouting warriors scrambled up to engage the fleeing Spaniards.

Crushed upon the narrow causeway, the Spaniards moved forward slowly, fighting all the way. It was a scene of horror. Cries of despair filled the air. At the gaps in the causeway, men and animals piled up. Cannons, baggage, war materials and Moctezuma's treasure were thrown into the murky waters to fill the gaps. Along the edges of the causeway men fought waist-deep in the water.

When near the second gap, Martín López was struck in the shoulder by an Indian arrow. He paused in pain and tried to break the ends of the arrow close to his flesh. While he was thus occupied, an Indian warrior crawled up the bank of the causeway, leaped upon him, dragging him down toward the water. Two other Indians in a canoe reached for him, trying to pull him aboard—a living offering for their sacrificial altar.

Suddenly, from above, a fury of sound and tan fur, a whirlwind of teeth and snarls, leaped into the boat. The attack by Martín's greyhound was so vicious the Indians dropped their prisoner to defend themselves. One of the warriors sank a dagger into the dog's heart, killing her. In that moment of respite Martín scrambled back up the bank, saving himself.

Although it seemed to Martín, faint from loss of blood from his wounds, that the horrors of the night would never end, at last the retreating column reached land. Soon the bitter Aztec attack let up. For a brief period the men were able to rest and to reorganize their battered forces.

Cortés restlessly hurried from group to group. Even though despair gripped the hearts of most of his men, he tried to cheer them up. He still believed he would conquer Mexico. He went among his men, anxiously asking about the fate of Martín López. When he learned that Martín was wounded, but was alive and safe, he showed great joy.

Bernadino Vasquez de Tápia, one of the soldiers who escaped across the causeway on that disastrous night, said of Cortés:

"Our Lord inspired Captain Cortés to believe that by means of Martín López this city which we now had lost would be regained. It was something we did not understand until much later."

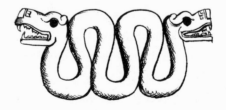

13 : The Navy That Crossed Mountains

During the long, dangerous retreat to Tlaxcala, Martín López entertained no thoughts of conquering the Aztecs. Like the rest of the men, he simply and desperately wanted to reach a place of safety where he could rest and heal his wounds. At times, he did not believe he would make it. Often, he saw his companions fall by the wayside. The wretched soldiers, faint from hunger and fatigue, dropped lifeless on the road. Some who were unable to keep up with the march fell into the hands of the enemy. Still others died in an unexpected and bitter battle with the Aztecs on the plains of Otumba.

Martín was especially grieved after this encounter because two of his closest friends were lost in it: the page boy, Orteguilla, and Pedro de Mafla, who had come with Martín from Sevilla. He also sorrowed over the loss of his faithful greyhound, who had given her life for Martín.

At last, the battered remnants of a once confident army reached Tlaxcala where these Indian allies welcomed them. Here Cortés counted his losses. In the long retreat he had lost almost two-thirds of his men. Among those who survived, every man had been wounded. He now had fewer than four hundred and fifty men. Only twenty of the more than one hundred horses had been saved. There were less than a dozen muskets left, and eleven crossbows. None of the cannons, powder nor amunition had been saved.

The men rested in Tlaxcala for twenty-two days. During this time Cortés and his lieutenants argued bitterly over what their next move should be. Would it be better to retreat to the coast and wait for help, or try to fight back from Tlaxcala?

"The only way we can return to Tenochtitlán is by ship," Martín López suggested. "Even if we have twenty thousand Indian allies, it won't help. We have seen how little room there is for our own men to maneuver on the causeways. Too many just get in each other's way. We need ships to protect the flanks of our soldiers on the causeways."

Cortés nodded. He had already realized this. In order to master Mexico he had to control Tenochtitlán and its valley. To do this he had to take advantage of the relationship between land and water, between the Aztec city and the lakes. Domination of the Aztec sea was the realistic road leading to the city.

"These are our tasks," he said. "First, control the

land and villages around the rim of the lake. Next, let us control the lake. Lastly, the city." He smiled at Martín, saying, "Master López, we need brigantines. Not merely four like those the Aztecs destroyed. We require a dozen or more."

"I can build them," Martín replied. "But you'll have to find a place to launch them from."

Cortés nodded. "You plan the ships," he said. "I'll find you a harbor."

After less than a month's rest in Tlaxcala, Cortés and his men struck back against the Aztecs. Some supplies had reached Villa Rica, and small contingents of men from the arriving ships joined Cortés. Throughout the summer a series of swift, stabbing campaigns were mounted and fought—an unbroken string of victories which tested the men and gave them new confidence. The object of the operations was to safeguard communications with Villa Rica and extend their control as far west as the edge of Lake Texcoco.

During the first months of the campaigns Martín fought with his companions. Realizing, however, that it would still take months before a beachhead could be established at Lake Texcoco, Martín hit upon a brilliant, time-saving idea. It was to prefabricate his ships in Tlaxcala, then transport them to the shore of Lake Texcoco once a base was established there.

The idea captivated Cortés. He used it to boost the

morale of his men. He called them together and made
a ceremony of giving Martín the shipbuilding orders.
"Master López," he said, "proceed to the city of Tlaxcala with your tools and everything necessary, and
seek a place where you can cut much wood—oak, ever-
green-oak and pine—and fashion it into the pieces
necessary to build thirteen brigantines."

Martín rounded up a larger crew of artisans than
he had had on any previous job. Among his helpers
were his cousin, Martinez Narices, Miguel de Mafla,
Andrés Nuñez, Alvar López, Diego de Hernandez,
Diego Ramírez, Francisco Rodriguez and Juan Gomez
de Herrera. These and other men—carpenters, cabinet-
makers, smiths and ironmongers—followed Martín
from Tepeaca, where Cortés had issued his order, to
Tlaxcala.

Since all the men were in their twenties, and preferred fighting to cutting wood, Martín used his imagination to make their work attractive. The men were
housed and handsomely cared for in the palace of
Macixca, one of the four Tlaxcalan chieftains. He had
Anton Codero serve as a caterer, foraging for supplies
and special foods, and seeing that everything was well
prepared. Lázaro Guerrero, who had been Martín's
friend both in Spain and Cuba, acted as purchasing
agent for the shipbuilders. He traveled back and forth
to the coast, picking up shipbuilding supplies, buying

cheeses and Spanish wines from the traders arriving by ship at Villa Rica.

For almost five months Martín's men worked on a project which, for its day, was a miracle. The task of building the ships was herculean because many of the supplies, the tools, metal and other gear were at a minimum. Timbers had to be hauled from great distances over rugged terrain.

Martín led groups of Indian workers to the distant slopes of the volcano, Malinche, and there marked off the best timber. The trees were cut and trimmed on the spot by the Indians. These were then hauled to the new shipyard on the banks of the Zahuapan River, a short distance upstream from the city of Tlaxcala.

On the banks of the stream the hum and activity of the shipyard broke the woodland silence. The sounds of sawing, hammering and the hissing of the forges filled the air as Indian carpenters did the crude dressing of the beams while Martín's men performed the close shaping and fitting. During the final weeks the men worked around the clock, and the scene was lit by candles, torches and bonfires.

When the dressed timbers, planks, masts, ironwork and other fittings were ready for final assembly, the ships were put together at the edge of the stream. This being February, the height of the dry season, a basin had to be created in which to float and test the hulls.

Martín supervised the work of more than five hundred Indians who built a dam across the river. The dam stood a little less than three miles above Tlaxcala, near the village of Tizatlán where today, more than four hundred years later, villagers still point out its earthen ramparts.

After completing the dam, the water level was allowed to rise so that four ships could be floated at a time. Although the masts and sails of the boats were stepped and mounted so as to check their balance, the superstructures of the vessels were not fixed in place.

During the tests, thousands of Tlaxcalans came to see the ships and marvel at their size. They were amazing spectacles, indeed, barkentines floating on a tiny stream locked in a forest valley. When the boats had been checked out, they were then taken apart. Each plank, beam, rudder and section was carefully brand-marked with a letter and a number so the vessels could be more easily reassembled at Lake Texcoco.

This cataloguing and marking was no easy task, because each ship was of a different size and shape. Although Martín had based his designs on the four lake brigantines constructed at Tenochtitlán, these he varied for different uses. In a dispatch sent to Cortés, he wrote: *Some should be small for pursuit duty, some large for ramming purposes.* It was an indication that Martín López was not merely a shipwright. He also understood naval tactics.

The vessels ranged in size from forty to forty-three feet in length. The flagship was forty-eight feet long. Like the lake brigantines, they were between seven and nine feet in beam, were shallow-draft and, at the waist, their freeboards measured about four feet, which contributed to their sailing qualities and combat convenience. Half of the boats were rigged with a single mast, half carried two masts. All had square-rigged sails. There was a low, center well-deck roomy enough for a row of oarsmen on each side and passage room for archers. The raised foredeck and poop deck were designed so that the Spanish gunners and archers towered above the Indian war canoes, as well as putting them at eye-level for action against Mexicans on the causeways. Some of the ships had reinforced bows for ramming enemy crafts.

While the shipbuilding went on in Tlaxcala, Martín López kept in constant touch with Cortés and followed the progress of the military operations. As the vessels were being tested in the river, word came that Cortés had captured the city of Texcoco. Martín was delighted.

Texcoco, lying at the eastern edge of Lake Texcoco, was the second largest city in the Aztec confederation.

It had once been an independent city-state, and it enjoyed the reputation of being the Athens of the empire. Its inhabitants were cultured and highly skilled. Cortés wrote that they were friendly to his cause. The city made an excellent base. There was excellent housing and it was easy to defend.

Martín rushed ahead with the preparations for moving his knock-down fleet to Texcoco. The magnitude of the job was fantastic. Thousands of tons of material, the timbers and planks, the unwieldy ribbings and shaped keels, the masts, yardages and sails, would have to be carried over seemingly impossible terrain.

Tlaxcala's mountain-locked shipyard lay more than sixty miles east of Texcoco, separated from the Aztec Athens by hostile country and towering mountains. Since draft animals and wheeled vehicles were unknown in the New World, Martín had to move his navy over the mountains upon the backs of men.

For this formidable task, he proved to be a master organizer. He assembled some fifty thousand Indian helpers to do the job. Thirty thousand of these were Tlaxcalan warriors led by their chieftains, who insisted on coming along to act as scouts and guards for the convoy.

Two thousand men were assigned the job of transporting the food needed on the trek. Eight thousand muscular porters were picked to carry the ship timbers and gear. Another nine thousand were held in reserve as relief porters.

After leaving Tlaxcala, the enormous van stopped to rest and wait for Gonzalo de Sandoval at the town of Hueyotlipán. When Sandoval joined them with the two hundred cavalrymen and infantry sent by Cortés, the huge column of more than fifty thousand men got underway once more. Sandoval, with eight horsemen, one hundred Spanish infantry, and a large body of Tlaxcalan warriors took the lead. The Indian carriers made up the middle of the van while more cavalry and infantry traveled along the flanks and as a rearguard.

The exact route taken by the spectacular ship-carrying convoy is no longer known. No written records have been found except those mentioning the stop at Hueyotlipán, and certain skirmishes with the enemy while en route. Undoubtedly the route followed was the one that offered the least difficult mountain barriers. From Hueyotlipán the convoy must have gone westward through the villages of Calpulalpan and Zoltepec, then passed slightly north of the high peak called Telapón.

The serpentine convoy, stretching out during the march for almost ten miles, single-filed through roadless terrain, crossing through a pass in a range of mountains that reached ten thousand feet into the clouds. Throughout the march Martín López raced

back and forth on horseback, keeping track of the various sections of his fleet, trying to keep the ranks as closed as possible. Sandoval's advance guard twice parried off enemy attempts to ambush and break up the convoy.

Finally, after three days of marching over rugged country without losing a man nor a piece of equipment, the convoy came within sight of Texcoco and the shimmering Aztec sea. At dawn on the fourth day the men prepared for a triumphal entry into Texcoco.

With banners flying, the Tlaxcalan warriors' feathers and finery brilliant in the morning sun, with trumpets blaring and drums rolling, the convoy moved toward the city. Never in the history of that city had so awesome a spectacle been witnessed. It took the procession six full hours to pass through the city's gates.

Cortés, his lieutenants and Father Olmeda came out to meet the convoy. Cortés threw his arms around Martín López in happy welcome. The two men rode into the city at the head of the column while their men shouted, "*Viva! Viva*, our King and Castile. *Viva* Castile and Tlaxcala. *Viva* Martín López."

The sound must have carried across the still waters of Lake Texcoco to the Aztecs in their island capital. The echo must have instilled fear. Martín López had fashioned a weapon to topple an empire.

14 : War in the Aztec Sea

Before Martín López had come to Texcoco he and Cortés had planned how the ships should be reassembled. Although Texcoco was situated a little more than a mile back from the lakeshore, it was decided to put the ships together in the city rather than locating the shipyard at the edge of the lake. This was done for security reasons. To set up the yards by the lake would have required a sizable round-the-clock guard of more crossbowmen, troops and artillery than Cortés could spare for this. He needed his men for operations in the field.

A few weeks before the convoy arrived at the city Cortés arranged to build a canal from the city to the lake so that when the ships were assembled they could be floated out. The Texcocoan chieftain, Ixitlilxochitl, a loyal supporter of the Spanish, was put in charge of this project.

Ixitlilxochitl was a remarkable engineer. He gathered about forty thousand Texcocoan laborers to work in shifts of eight thousand men at a time. In seven weeks they cut a canal through solid rock and broken ground. The channel was over twelve feet deep at its shipyard end within the city. It measured about ten to twelve feet across. Ixitlilxochitl also devised a series of intricate locks and water pumps so the depth of the water in the canal could be varied as needed.

Today, there is no trace of the canal in modern Texcoco, but it is said to have begun at a point where there now stands a monument and a plaque that reads:

Bridge of the Brigantines
Where Cortés launched the ships
For the siege
Of the Aztec Capital.

The day after his arrival in Texcoco, Martín López had his canal-side shipyard humming. His Tlaxcalan crew, and some new men—Melchor de Alabes, Juan Ramos de Lares and Juan García—speedily began assembling the hulls, fitting planks, trunnels and bolts.

The detail work was enormous. The pumps had to be tested, the ship bottoms treated, the sails hung, the rudders, pendants and tillers positioned. Masts had to be properly stepped, the spars fixed and the cordage put in smooth operating order. The ramming reinforcements had to be checked. Cannons were securely bolted to the decks.

Calking the hulls was a problem. Every seam had to be sealed carefully with material that would last, because once the ships were in action there would be no time for them to return to their dry docks. In his chronicle of the conquest, Bernal Díaz mentions that human fat from victims of the Indian sacrificial altars was used for calking the ships. This is most doubtful. Both Cortés and Ixitlilxochitl forbade human sacrifice in Texcoco. Furthermore, among the Martín López records there are notes saying that before leaving Tlaxcala, Hernando de Aguilar and four sailors were sent to the pine forests near the town of Guaxalcingo to secure great quantities of pitch for calking the vessels.

While the ships were being assembled Cortés and his men launched an intense campaign, fighting their way around the lake, capturing villages which might be used later as bases.

At the same time, the Aztecs were preparing their defenses. Following the death of Moctezuma, and the expulsion of the Spaniards from Tenochtitlán, the Aztecs had suffered a temporary disorganization which had prevented them from attacking the Spaniards when the latter were at their weakest. The people had been ravaged by smallpox, a disease brought to the New World by one of Narvaez' crewmen. The epidemic caused countless deaths and suffering. Even Moctezuma's successor had died of the disease.

Now, the Aztecs were strong once more. They had a new leader, the celebrated Cuauhtemoc, a nephew of Moctezuma. He was about twenty-five years old, and was a handsome, well-built young man, with a complexion somewhat lighter than that of the average Aztec. He was a fine athlete and an exceptionally courageous warrior.

Unlike Moctezuma, Cuauhtemoc knew what had to be done. He did not believe that the Spaniards were gods. He also rejected the ancient prophecies and omens predicting the fall of Tenochtitlán. His positive attitude unified and inspired his followers. He had his people fortify their city. He sent spies into Texcoco and to Villa Rica to keep him informed of the reinforcements and supplies Cortés was receiving.

His agents had warned him of the ships being built in Tlaxcala. He realized how dangerous the ships could be. He made a number of attempts to destroy them. While the boats were being assembled at Texcoco three strong raiding parties were sent across the lake to set them on fire. Unfortunately for Cuauhtemoc, Spanish vigilance was such that the attacking parties were repulsed.

On Saturday night, April 27, 1521, Martín López

informed Cortés that the thirteen brigantines were ready. He would launch them the next day. Early Sunday morning Ixitlilxochitl signaled for the pumps and waterwheels to turn, bringing the water in the locks up to the required level. Then, one by one, the ships were run down the canal and launched in the waters of Lake Texcoco.

It was a gala day for Spain, for Cortés, and for Martín López. The ships were anchored near shore while Father Olmeda, dressed in his liturgical vestments, celebrated Mass, then went about blessing each vessel—the first real navy constructed on the American continent. The Spaniards, all of the inhabitants of Texcoco as well as thousands of Tlaxcalan allies, lined the shore for the celebration.

As the good friar blessed each ship, the sails were unfurled and banners fluttered from the riggings and masts. Music burst forth and there were repeated salutes fired from the cannons on the foredeck of each ship. The cries, the *vivas*, the outpouring of emotions, was so great that men who had fought in dozens of battles and were hardened to wounds wept for joy over this fleet which Martín López had created in less than eight months.

Cortés made a speech praising Martín and his ships. In passionate tones he cried out, *"Los bergantines, la llave de toda la guerra."* ("These brigantines are the key to the war.")

Although no one standing along the beach thought of it at the time, the creation of the fleet and the success of the Spanish conquest in Mexico were due to the fact that Cortés' men were not professional soldiers. Though a few had fought in the Italian wars, most were artisans—ranchers, sailors, blacksmiths, carpenters and shipwrights. They pooled their civilian talents to make possible a military victory.

Though a fleet was launched, and rode majestically on the glistening waters of the Aztec sea, it was not yet a navy. The crews and fighting men had to be trained.

All the Spaniards were pleased that this new weapon had been forged. However, many of the men did not care to serve on the ships. Some of them felt that there was nothing romantic about manning the oars of an oversize galley. They much preferred to be fighting men. Although some volunteered to serve on the ships, Cortés and Martín López had to comb through their records, noting which men had been sailors before coming to Mexico, who had been a fisherman, who had lived in a port town.

It was easier to select the ship commanders. Instead

of appointing sea captains and pilots to the top command of the vessels, Cortés picked some of his most experienced military lieutenants. His reason for this was sound. The navy would not be employed as were most navies of that day—to fight naval engagements or pursue pirates. The principal task of the fleet would be to support the infantry fighting along the causeways to Tenochtitlán. The ships were to be a seagoing cavalry.

Martín López was made assistant captain on the flagship or *capitana*, but after the first engagement with the enemy, when Captain Juan Rodriguez de Villafuerte abandoned ship, Martín took over. A little later he was put in charge of fleet operations and became Cortés' admiral of the fleet.

Other ship commanders were Pedro Barba, Antonio de Caravajal, García Holguín, Pedro Briones, Miguel Díaz de Aux, Juan Jaramillo, Cristóbal Flores, Rodrigo Morejón, Andrés Nuñez, Juan Portillo, Francisco Verdugo and Antonio Sotello.

The crews of each boat included a captain; a second in command, who was usually a seaman; twelve sailors who handled the sails and could row when there was no wind. On each vessel there was a company of twelve crossbowmen, musketeers and artillerymen who were exempt from rowing.

Before going into action the fleet made a number of

shakedown cruises along the southeastern edge of the lake until the men and ships had learned to work in unison. Toward the end of May, Martín advised Cortés that the fleet was ready.

The brigantines were not the only naval force at Cortés' disposal. It was known that Cuauhtemoc had assembled an enormous fleet of war canoes and pirogues. These ranged from canoes holding two men, to large pirogues that carried fifty warriors. In all, Cuauhtemoc had more than fifty thousand boats available. With these he planned to surround the Spanish fleet and destroy it. His canoes would swarm over it like ants over a dead beetle. To oppose this armada of canoes, Martín López and Cortés brought together a fleet of about sixteen thousand canoes manned by fifty thousand Texcocoan paddlers and warriors. Chief Ixitlilxochitl was put in command of the Indian flotilla.

During the last week of May, Cortés, his lieutenants and the Texcocoan chieftains held several war councils to assign operations and iron out their strategy. By now, Cortés had built up his Spanish fighting force to about six hundred and forty men. More than half, or about three hundred and twenty-five men, were assigned to the navy. The fleet had the bulk of the crossbowmen, musketeers and artillery.

The land force was divided into three mobile units, one for each of the principal causeways leading across the lake to Tenochtitlán. Pedro de Alvarado, Cristóbal de Olid and Gonzalo de Sandoval were the commanders. Between them they had eighty-four horsemen, fifty-five bowmen and musketeers and over four hundred foot soldiers, and a great number of Indian warriors.

Cortés' strategy for reducing the Aztec capital was simple. He planned to combine blockade, siege and assault. The three land units were ordered to occupy the causeways, cutting Cuauhtemoc's land communications with his empire. The navy would clear the Aztec sea of native boats and set up a tight blockade, preventing canoe-borne food and supplies from reaching the city. Then, after Tenochtitlán's defenders were weakened by starvation and thirst, the direct assault would begin.

Before sunrise, the last day of May, the land forces set out from Texcoco. At daybreak Cortés boarded the navy's flagship. A blare of trumpets signaled the sailors to lift anchors.

Under sail and paddle the ships moved toward the long Netzahualcóyotl Dike which extended from the northern rim of the lake to its southern shore. The dike had given Martín López considerable worry. He had feared that the Aztecs might fill in the gaps in this extensive stone barrier, thus bottling his ships in the eastern half of the lake where they could not help the troops on the causeways. For some unknown reason the Aztecs missed this golden opportunity.

Slowly, the fleet filed through the dike passages and sailed into the main body of the lake—enemy waters. The navy's first objective was a high, rock point, the Peñon de Tepepolco, which stood in the lake about three miles from the town of Iztapalapa. The Peñon was an important prize because the Aztecs used it as a lookout point and signal tower.

The guns of the brigantines scattered the few enemy boats lurking around the Peñon. An assault party from the ships stormed the beach and, after a brisk battle, took the point. It was America's first amphibious assault.

Cortés and Martín López climbed to the crest of the Peñon. They remained there but a moment. From this dizzy perch they spied an enormous flotilla of Aztec boats approaching from Tenochtitlán. Hurrying back to the brigantines, they gave the signal to proceed and meet the enemy.

It was now early afternoon, a brilliant, sunny day. As the brigantines moved out into the lake the breeze suddenly died. The ships, difficult to maneuver by paddle alone, were becalmed. The sails drooped and the vessels lost mobility. The lighter Indian canoes came on swiftly until they were within an arrow's flight of the Spanish boats. Then the Indian boats stopped.

As the two naval forces, Aztec and Spanish, lay on the still waters, two widely different cultures faced each other. The ships lay still while tension grew. Each side waited for the other to move first. Beneath the hypnotic, vertical rays of the Mexican sun, the suspense became unbearable.

Martín López watched the sails and pennants of his ship hang motionless in the listless air. Meanwhile, more and more war canoes came from Tenochtitlán until the waters were black with them.

Martín prayed desperately. "Unless a miracle occurs, they'll sweep over us like a tidal wave."

15 : The Fall of Tenochtítlán

A n hour of incredible tension slipped by while the
Aztec flotilla, representing the might of the Indian world, faced the becalmed and helpless Spanish
fleet.

Then the miracle Martín López had prayed for
occurred. A breeze suddenly blew out of the south-
west, fluttering the pennants overhead. As the breeze
stiffened the sails bellied, scooping wind from the sky.
A shout of triumph rang out aboard the ships. Cortés
ordered the trumpeter to sound the signal for fleet
action.

Picking up speed, the brigantines scudded over the
water under full sail and bore down upon the massed
enemy war canoes. The Aztecs were so surprised they
scarcely fired an arrow. They tried to turn their boats
and flee, but it was too late. Brigantine after brigantine
rammed into the pirogues, running them down and
sinking them. The bowmen, musketeers and cannoneers fired repeated salvos, creating terrible havoc. The

lake was covered with wreckage and tinted with the blood of the enemy.

The *capitana,* on which Cortés and Martín López sailed, pursued two large Aztec pirogues. Suddenly the barkentine grounded on a hidden reef. Seeing that the flagship was helpless, the Aztec boats turned to attack it. When the first Indian warriors leaped aboard the ship, Captain Rodriguez de Villafuerte jumped overboard in panic. Some of the crewmen followed him. Martín López and Cortés dropped to the well-deck and furiously fought with the Aztecs until they had cleared the ship. While the bowmen and gunners held off the enemy, Martín and his seamen refloated the vessel.

By this time, the Texcocoan canoes under Ixitlilxochitl had joined in the battle. In less than an hour the naval battle was over. The magnitude of the victory was spectacular. Cortés had secured control of the Aztec sea. He was so pleased, he announced to all the men aboard the flagship, "This is the best and greatest victory we could have asked or desired. Master López' ships are truly our key to victory."

The destruction of the Aztec flotilla was not the last of the day's successes. In the afternoon the fleet sailed westward toward the Iztapalapa causeway. Now, Cortés' objective was the Indian fortress of Acachinanco straddling the causeway midway between Tenochtitlán and the southern shore of the lake.

The brigantines sailed in close to the causeway and its fortified buildings. Like a modern navy, the brigantines laid down a barrage of cannon fire. Then, with the late afternoon sun almost blinding them, thirty men plunged into the water and scrambled up the stone sides of the causeway. The surprised defenders, expecting a Spanish assault along the causeway from the south, were quickly overcome.

Having easily captured this key position, Cortés had four cannons put ashore to defend the fort. He decided to make it his headquarters, as well as the advance base for the entire fleet. He sent instructions to Cristóbal de Olid to bring up his cavalry and infantry. The fleet had saved Olid the task of fighting his way up the causeway and storming the fort.

While the cannons were being set up in the fort, a careless Spanish soldier set fire to the powder supply. Cortés dispatched one of the smaller, swift brigantines to Sandoval's land unit, requesting more powder. It was a dramatic example of the use of the navy for supply duty and liason, as well as for fighting.

The most important point brought home to the Spanish by the day's operations was that their ships could be used as cavalry, to strike swiftly, to divide and conquer. The fleet gave them a mobility they had not enjoyed before. They could assault positions behind the enemy lines. They could strike swiftly in places the enemy least expected it.

In spite of this new advantage, and the confidence it gave Cortés' men, the siege of Tenochtitlán occupied almost ninety days. It was no easy task for a small body of men and their Indian allies to topple an empire and crush a strongly fortified city that was defended by hundreds of thousands of valiant people.

Cortés' three columns of infantry and cavalry stubbornly pushed their way along the causeways to the edge of the city. During this period, men had to be shifted from the operation against the city to wage several campaigns elsewhere in the valley when supporters of Cuauhtemoc threatened the Spanish rearguard and supply bases.

While these operations were in progress, the navy, commanded by Martín López, continued to play a vital role.

The fleet was divided into squadrons which patrolled both sides of each causeway, warding off the remnants of Cuauhtemoc's canoes attempting to harry the Spaniards fighting toward the city. The ships made it possible for the men on the causeways to rest each night without fear of being surprised by a canoe-borne attack.

On more than one occasion the brigantines served as

bridges. When Sandoval's troops had trouble crossing a gap in the Mexicaltzingo section of the main causeway where the Aztecs had destroyed the bridge, Martín López sailed two brigantines, side by side, into the gap, thus turning his ships into a handy pontoon bridge.

In addition to cruising day and night about the lake, clearing the waters of enemy war canoes as well as the thousands of small canoes that normally carried foodstuffs to the city, the brigantines carried the war into Tenochtitlán long before land troops reached the city. On the second day of the campaign a squadron of brigantines probed the canals at the edge of the city.

The Aztecs so feared the brigantines, realizing that unless the ships were destroyed they were lost, that they made desperate attempts to capture them. One day they devised an elaborate ambush. Thirty large war pirogues were camouflaged in the reeds along the shore of the lake. Stakes were driven in the shallows to snag the brigantines. Toward evening a group of swift canoes skirted within sight of the brigantines to act as bait. When Martín's ships gave chase, the canoes swerved toward the shore where the war pirogues were hidden. All at once, the pirogues broke out of their camouflage and surrounded the Spanish squadron.

Although most of the squadron managed to escape, the ambush cost Martín's navy dearly. During the fighting, Juan Portillo, a brigantine captain, was killed. Pedro Barba, the commander of another ship, was mortally wounded and died shortly afterward. His brigantine was captured by the Indians and burned. A number of his crewmen were also taken, and sacrificed.

A few days later, Martín López staged a similar ambush, destroying over one hundred Indian boats.

By mid-July the brigantines and Texcocoan boats had cleared the lake of canoes, and the combined land and naval blockade was tightening around the doomed city. Spanish brigantines and Ixitlilxochitl's canoes were penetrating deeply into the city. Pedro de Alvarado's men had advanced over the causeway and were fighting from house to house in the northern section of the city.

Despite the increasing fatigue from so long a campaign, both sides battled with bitter determination. Cuauhtemoc's followers fought out of desperation—men with their backs to the wall. The Spaniards fought with another kind of desperation—fear of the sacrificial altars.

Many of the Spanish soldiers, as well as their Tlaxcalan and Texcocoan allies, had fallen into the hands of the Aztecs. Day and night, the huge ceremonial war drum on the principal Aztec temple sounded its ominous voice. It was like a continual dirge announcing the death of brave men upon the altars. The Spaniards, fighting within the city, helplessly watched their companions being sacrificed.

In the second week of August the entire Spanish force seized control of the Tlatelolco, or northern half of the city, which was separated from the center by a wide canal. Cortés tried to negotiate with Cuauhtemoc. When the peace talks failed, the Spaniards attempted to bombard the Aztecs into surrendering.

The engine used for this maneuver was the brainchild of a soldier named Sotello, who claimed to be an engineer. He said he had seen catapults destroy whole cities in the Italian wars. Martín López' cousin, Juan Martinez Narices, and a group of carpenters built the war machine according to Sotello's instructions.

The machine, constructed of heavy timbers, tension ropes, and slings designed to fling rocks the size of four gallon jugs, was set in place. Sotello took charge. When the slings were loaded and ready to fire, Sotello gave the signal. The catapult worked well. The huge rocks went straight up in the air. But instead of arching toward Cuauhtemoc's stronghold, the stones fell back, crashing on the pavement beside the catapult.

Although Cortés was very angry with Sotello over this failure, all the other Spaniards who had gathered around to watch the wonderful bombardment burst into laughter. It was the first time the battle-weary men had laughed in months.

The assault on Cuauhtemoc's section of the city was resumed with fury. On the morning of August 13, 1521, when the Spaniards finally crossed the wide canal, it seemed as though the war would end with the capture of Cuauhtemoc's palace. Instead, the war ended on the lake.

That morning Martín López and Sandoval were aboard the flagship, patrolling along the southeast edge of the city. A short distance from them, García Holguín, commanding a smaller, swifter brigantine, suddenly spied a fleet of fifty large pirogues leaving the high reeds for deep water. Two of the Indian boats were rigged out in a royal fashion, having colored cotton awnings to shade the occupants.

Holguín's barkentine and the flagship turned in pursuit of the Indian flotilla. Holguín's vessel, being the swifter, soon outdistanced Martín's flagship and captured the canopy-covered Indian boat. His prize was the Aztec leader, Cuauhtemoc.

Even today, no one knows whether the Aztec leader was fleeing from the city, planning to carry on the war from the mainland, or, as some historians claim, was on his way to surrender to Cortés in order to spare his people further suffering. In any event, the capture of Cuauhtemoc abruptly ended the war. The last decisive event in Spain's conquest of Mexico was a naval action.

16 : Afterward

For days after the collapse of Aztec resistance, Spanish squads patrolled through the rubble of a once fabulous city.

Martín López was shocked by the havoc that had been done. He wandered through the streets, sadly remembering how it had looked when he had first set eyes on the city less than two years before. Now, scarcely a house remained in good condition. The vivid gardens were all destroyed. Even those houses that remained were being razed and burned to prevent the spread of disease.

The streets, the royal palaces and plazas of Tenochtitlán were so filled with bodies of the dead it was almost impossible to pass through them. And among the dead, the Spaniards found men and women who, though still alive, were too starved to stand or move. In its death throes, Tenochtitlán had resisted bravely. Her men had fought longer and more valiantly than seemed possible. For weeks the defenders had been without fresh water. There had been no food brought in for more than a month. The people had lived on roots dug up in their gardens.

For three days and nights after the fall of the city all the causeways, once scenes of bitter battles, were crowded with emaciated men, women and children abandoning their city. They fled toward the mainland where food and shelter might be found.

Since the city was no longer habitable, the Spaniards made their headquarters at Coyoacan, a tree-shaded village on the southern shore of the lake. There they brought their important prisoners: Cuauhtemoc and his lords, and also the son of Moctezuma who had been captured by Ixitlilxochitl.

Some days after the destruction of the city, Cortés gave a victory banquet for his men. A ship from Spain had arrived at Villa Rica, bringing fine wines, cheeses and Spanish hams for the festival. According to Bernal Díaz, the banquet became a very noisy, confused affair. Men drank the good wines, ate too much and, like soldiers everywhere, they argued about the battles they had fought in. Sandoval and Holguín disputed with one another as to who should have had the honor of delivering Cuauhtemoc to Cortés.

Since these men had fulfilled a dream, conquering an opulent empire, they talked loudly of the things they hoped to get out of their victory. The cavalrymen spoke of buying beautiful stallions outfitted with golden saddles. The crossbowmen dreamed of arrows and golden quivers.

Martín López dreamed of returning to Sevilla, of seeing his family, of basking in glory. Perhaps he might become a great sea captain. Fascinated by his role as Cortés' naval commander, he discussed naval strategy with Father Olmeda. The priest, a well-read and brilliant man, compared the naval victories in the Aztec sea to the battle at Salamis between the Athenian and Persian navies which had decided the fate of two civilizations.

But neither Martín nor Father Olmeda really understood the full significance of their victory on the more than mile-high Aztec sea. The fall of Tenochtitlán would be remembered as the only naval war that ended both a war and a civilization. A whole Indian world had been overturned and crushed.

And, of course, neither man completely understood how this had happened. During Cortés' various campaigns the Indians had quickly accustomed themselves to each new weapon which had given the Spaniards a momentary advantage. The Indians had lost their fear of the horses. They devised ways of coping with the cannons and muskets. But the creation of Martín López' navy provided the Spaniards with a weapon the Indians had no defense against. It gave Cortés a psychological weapon without which no victory would have been possible. For the Indians, the brigantines were a nightmare come to life. They were the key to the conquest. Once Mexico was taken, Spain was able to rapidly dominate the rest of Central America and South America.

What happened to Martín López after the conquest? Like the crossbowmen at the victory banquet, did he dream of treasures, of a golden brigantine? Did he return to Sevilla as a hero? Did he become a famous sea captain?

After the fall of Tenochtitlán, Martín lived in Mexico for more than a half-century. He saw Mexico City rise like a phoenix from the ashes of the Aztec capital. From time to time, the yearning for further adventures bit him. He went on an expedition to the Panuco River; he accompanied Nuño de Gúzman on a two-year exploration of Nueva Galicia—the northern region that now includes part of Arizona, New Mexico and Chihuahua.

In 1528 he had a disagreement with Hernando Cortés. Although Cortés had named his first son, Martín, as time went by he seemed to have forgotten his debt to Martín López. Cortés had grown wealthy, powerful and autocratic. He had shared few benefits and little of his wealth with men like Martín. Egged on by friends, Martín López sued Cortés in court, demanding eight thousand pesos as payment for his labor and his personal funds which he had spent in constructing the brigantines. Although many of the men who had helped build the brigantines at Tlaxcala came forward as witnesses, the suit was unsuccessful.

At about this time, Martín fell in love with a Spanish girl who had come to Mexico with her parents. In 1534 he married her in Mexico City. For a while he and his wife lived at Tehuantepec, in the far south, where he held a government post. A little later the Spanish government awarded him land and a half of a town to rule over in the region of Tequixquiac. He and his shipbuilding companion, Andrés Nuñez, tried to make a go of this, but the region was very poor. The two men and their wives struggled to exist.

In the 1550's Martín returned to Mexico City with his family, which now included four girls and four boys. During the remainder of his life he seemed to swing between poverty and moments of fairly good living.

Even in old age he could never really rest. The vivid adventures of the conquest had left their imprint on him. At nights the roar of cannons and muskets, the shrill war cries of Indians, the dismal beat of the great war drum on the Aztec temple, echoed in his ears. Like his companions in war, he had grown so accustomed to alertness, to sleeping on hard floors and the earth, with his weapons ready, that he kept this habit in the years after. He could never sleep well on a mattress. He could only sleep for short periods at night. He often rose, walked about, listened for strange sounds, or watched the moon gleaming in the night sky like a silver Aztec amulet.

Sometimes he went down through the new city, along a street called Calle de los Bergantines, to the waterfront. After the fall of Tenochtitlán, Cortés had established a fort at the water-edge, where the brigantines were safe from attack yet could sail out to patrol the lake. The fort had two strong towers with loopholes, and the towers were connected by arched naves beneath which the ships could be anchored. After some years most of the brigantines were taken apart. Some of their beams and planks were used in the construction of a monastery, called the Merced, built on the site of the fort. In modern times, this became the area of Mexico City's vast central market.

The exact date of Martín López' death is not known. According to records, he was still alive and in Mexico City as late as 1573. There are no known records of where he was buried.

It is strange that the only tangible reward Martín López received for his important role in the conquest of Mexico was a coat of arms from the King of Spain. The shield had thirteen brigantines shown on it. For

years after Martín's death his children's families continued displaying this coat of arms.

But who remembers Martín López? Today, if you
drive in your car across the dry bed of the Aztec sea—
a part of it is now Mexico's international airport—and
you come to a certain traffic light in the city, exactly
at a point where four hundred years ago water lapped
against the stone docks of Tenochtitlán, you can look
up and see a street sign that reads, CALLE LOPEZ.

If you ask anyone in the shops along the street
whether they know who Martín López was, you'll
probably be answered with a puzzled shrug. Although
the siege of Tenochtitlán was one of the most extraordinary naval operations in history, mirroring the
future of naval wars—blockades, coordinated naval and
land operations, marine landings and a unique naval
action in the heart of a great city—no one on López
Avenue knows anything about the man who designed
the navy, and chalked up so many remarkable "firsts"
in the annals of adventure.

BRIEF BIBLIOGRAPHY

The Martín López Documents, G.R.G. Conway Collection, U.S. Library of Congress.

The True History of the Conquest of New Spain, Bernal Díaz, Doubleday.

The Conquest of Mexico, William H. Prescott.

Historical Works, Fernando de Alva Ixitlilxochitl.

Letters Related to the Conquest of Mexico, Hernando Cortés.

Naval Power in the Conquest of Mexico, C. Harvey Gardiner, University of Texas Press.

From the Viewpoint of the Conquered, University of Mexico Press. A collection of Indian documents.

The Author

JAMES NORMAN resides in Mexico, and has been a student of the Conquistadores and early civilizations of Mexico. Earlier, as a newspaper reporter he covered Europe during the explosive years that led to World War II. During the war he served as a combat correspondent in the Pacific Theatre, and earned the Bronze Star on Luzon in the Philippines. Although now living in Mexico, he returns to the United States frequently and maintains his American citizenship.